Exhaling
the Gospel
of Jesus Christ

Exhaling
the Gospel
of Jesus Christ

Evangelism as Natural as
Breathing the Truth

Dan Allen

Published in Allentown, Pennsylvania.

Published in association with 800FollowMe.com

ISBN 978-0-692-27849-9

Printed in the United States of America

17 18 19 20 — 9 8 7 6 5 4 3

Dedication

to

Rev. Russell T. Allen
(1929-1979)

&

Rev. Joshua M. Allen
(1983-2014)

Contents

Endorsements

"In this excellent guide to personal evangelism, Dan Allen presents numerous practical ideas how to relate to those who need new life in Christ. *Exhaling the Gospel of Jesus Christ* makes sharing the Gospel as natural as breathing. I heartily recommend this helpful volume to anyone who longs to be an effective witness."

Dr. Ronald Blue
Professor, Dallas Theological Seminary;
Past President of CAM International

"R.A. Torrey said – 'I'd like to ask what right a man has to call himself a follower of Jesus if he is not a soul-winner.' I feel my good friend Dan Allen in his book *Exhaling the Gospel of Jesus Christ* has provided an invaluable tool for the person who desires to share the Gospel. This book Exposes you to the great need – Exhorts you to be a witness for Christ – Excites you to see what God will do in a life. Read this book and you will be excited to "gossip the Gospel!"

Dr. Wendell Calder
Director, Local Church Evangelism

"Dan Allen combines a scholar's mind with a pastor's heart to provide today's church with an incredible new evangelism tool that will ignite your church with a passion to fulfill the Great Commission.

Dr. Ed Hindson
Dean & Distinguished Professor of Religion,
Liberty University

"The substance of this book concerns matters of seriousness and weightiness, matters of eternal consequence and destiny. Yet, on the whole, it has a certain lightheartedness about it, that makes it actually fun to read, easy to engage, and enjoyable to interact with. Sprinklings of humor help sweeten the still-substantive message. Turns out that's the point. Sharing the message of Jesus does not have to be uncomfortable or off-putting. Those of us who have had the privilege of knowing the author personally can testify that this book also reflects his own practice, character, and manner authentically — a real plus. In fact, that may make all the difference."

Dr. Todd Mangum
Professor of Theology, Academic Dean,
Biblical Theological Seminary

"To know Dan Allen as I have for 30 years is to know a man who carefully handles Scripture with accuracy and clarity. His high regard for truth flows through his book on personal evangelism with a combination of grace for each one of us trying to become better at sharing our faith, and grace for those we seek to reach with the gospel. Dan has always demonstrated this rare balance by practicing what he consistently teaches."

Dr. Peter Teague
President, Lancaster Bible College

"When it comes to evangelism, it's easy to make people feel guilty. I'm glad to report that Dan Allen has written a book that makes me say, 'Hey! I could do that. *Exhaling the Gospel of Jesus Christ* combines wise biblical insight with practical tools that will enable you to share Christ with your friends and neighbors. The good news is, you really can do this and Dan Allen shows you how."

Dr. Ray Pritchard
Director, Keep Believing Ministries

"Dan Allen is a Christian leader of remarkable depth, creativity, and integrity. He is now entering a new phase of his life as an author. What a subject he has chosen! How does one share his faith naturally and without embarrassment? One cannot really walk with Jesus without lifting Him up and sharing His supreme beauty, attractiveness, and pre-eminence. Dan, in this fine, short book shows each of us how to share his faith without anxiety and fear. He and his wife, Vonnie, have had their faith purified and tempered in the furnace of suffering, loss, and shock. Their son, Josh, fellow minister of the Gospel, recently lost his life in a tragic accident. This has been exceedingly difficult and life-changing, but it has also brought a marvelous, spiritual reality and depth to both of their lives. Trusting Jesus which is the theme of this book, is like breathing. It is keeping them alive. Breathing and trusting will keep us alive as well!

Dr. Don Wyrtzen
Composer and author

Forward

Dan Allen is a graduate of Liberty University and I appreciate all he has done for Christ in so many different areas of ministry. Then his son Josh Allen, who graduated from Liberty University also was my graduate assistant and grader. It was Josh who kept me updated on what Dan was doing for Christ.

I have read the manuscript "Exhaling The Gospel of Jesus Christ," and appreciate its human approach to the gospel. So often the plan of salvation is presented from a divine prospective, i.e., what God has done. Dan Allen has presented what man must do in response to the great salvation and commission offered by Jesus Christ. It is a great book and I pray that God will use it in many ways.

Josh Allen, Dan's son, took over a new church plant in New Mexico. He was presenting the gospel to many unsaved people in an attempt to reach the lost of the area. Josh was carrying on the ministry of his father (and grandfather), both carrying on the ministry they learned at Liberty University.

On February 24, 2014, Josh Allen was killed instantly when a car drove down the wrong way on a very busy interstate in Texas. I was so saddened by the news, and was not able to attend Josh's funeral, but sent words of appreciation for Josh's ministry and recorded a memorial on video of appreciation of Josh's ministry.

It is unusual for the son to go first, usually it is the father that goes first, but in this case God has left Dan Allen to carry on the ministry of evangelism. He not only will do this in person, but he will do it through the book, "Exhaling The Gospel of Jesus Christ." May God bless and use this book as a catalyst to win many people to Christ.

Dr. Elmer Towns
Co-Founder & Vice President, Liberty University
(Short Bio on Elmer Towns, page 177)

Introduction

Writing about the greatest story ever told, concerning the greatest Person to ever live and the greatest gift ever offered, requires a person of letters, someone who is a great writer. That person is not me.

Writing never come easily to me. It's easier now, but when I first started it was laborious.

Not so with my dad. Rev. Russell T. Allen was able to write at the drop of a hat – or purse. (His description in an article of what was in his wife's purse, when he accidently dumped it, was priceless). In addition to weekly and monthly articles, he completed one book (*Over the River to Charlie*, a short biography on the "prince of preachers," Charles Haddon Spurgeon) and had several others on the drawing board before his untimely death at the age of 50. He also could write in verse. His poem "I'm Home Now," written for one of his parishioners who passed away, has been read at countless Christian funerals and memorial services. As a tribute to my dad and for your benefit and encouragement, I've included it at the end of the book (page 183).

Following in my father's footsteps as a pastor, I assumed I'd have to pick up a pen. Writing must be required, I thought. It's not, but I didn't know that then. And was it ever difficult! First, I couldn't think of things about which to write—not to mention I had a full preaching load (Sunday morning and evening plus Sunday School and Wednesday night sermons) as well as all the pastoral duties expected of ministers.

Then I started observing my surroundings more closely. I attempted to explain what I was seeing and experiencing. The children came along and provided a treasure-trove of ideas. Experiences in the church and community, as well as national and international happenings, added to the supply.

Stringing words together in a coherent piece that was interesting was the second problem. It seemed like hours tapping a pencil eraser to the desk trying to express my thoughts. But I soldiered on to complete something. I also made a commitment to myself and to God: I vowed to write an article each week so that when I finally had something important to say, I'd know how to say it.

Thirty-some years later, I have something important to say. It's this book. It's this venture into personal evangelism. Due to various ministry circumstances I have been afforded the time my dad was never granted to focus solely on one subject. The result is what you are holding in your hands as well as "The Nathanael Project" (see page 184).

You should know that I do not come at this subject as an expert. I don't believe I have the gift of evangelism. I do the "work of an evangelist" (1 Tim. 4:12) in my calling as a pastor, but I'm a pilgrim like you. I struggle to gain the courage to speak up about my Lord. I have the same fears you do about failing. It's equally hard for me to discern to whom I should go, when I should start, and how. But I have found that, as in writing, the more I share my faith, the more I talk to people about the hope within me (1 Pet. 3:15), the more confident I become and the easier it seems. This doesn't mean I should stop learning techniques on how better to witness. It's a continual process, and I'm growing.

I remember one of the first letters-to-the-editor I wrote to the local paper. It was early in my ministry. Some local issue had rung a bell, and I was fired up. I sat at the old typewriter, before computers and spell-check (which became dreadfully obvious), and pecked away. The letter appeared in the next week's paper, and, to my horror, it had an editor's note right after it stating the letter had been entered as it had been received – mistakes and all. I was mortified. I thought editors were supposed to—you know, EDIT! Not according to that grizzled old newspaper man. The editor, with whom I developed a good working relationship for a number of years until his untimely death, taught me a valuable lesson. Not only do I need a proofreader (I have two for everything I write), but I must constantly hone my craft.

Introduction

The purpose of this book, via some New Testament stories, is to help us sharpen our skills in fulfilling what we have been mandated to do – present the Good News of Jesus Christ (Matthew 28:19-20). In a non-confrontational, loving manner, we need to tell our relatives, friends, co-workers and neighbors about Jesus Christ and how He loved them so much He paid the price so that they can have the gift of eternal life. This needs to flow from us as naturally as we breathe. It should be second nature.

If you're a seasoned soul-winner, I trust the Holy Spirit will use something in this short book to sharpen your witnessing skills and encourage you to keep at it. For the newbie, I'm praying the Holy Spirit will not only convince you that you can do this, but that you must!

Let's soldier on together as we write new chapters of God's amazing grace being imparted to your friends and mine.

Dan Allen
October 2014
February 2017

1

Brush With the Greatest
As Simple As An Introduction
John 1:43-51

Phil had to tell Nate. He was so excited about a recent "brush with greatness" that his friend, Nathanael, needed to have the same encounter.

If you've ever run into a celebrity, you might know how Philip felt. Maybe you were at an airport and a professional athlete with his entourage walked right by you. Perhaps it was a movie star, a world famous musician, or even a popular or unpopular politician. The first thing you did after doing a double-take to make sure it was really "them," and shaking off the goose bumps, was to notify everyone you know. "You'll never guess who I just saw!" If you're fortunate enough to get a selfie with the star, it's downloaded and uploaded in the blink of an eye.

We are social creatures and, as such, need to tell others the good, the bad, and the ugly of our lives. If we have a "brush with greatness," everyone must know.

That must be how Philip felt about his encounter with the Messiah.

The story about Philip and Nathanael is recorded in the first chapter of John's Gospel (1:43-51). After identifying who Jesus Christ is—the Word—and presenting the testimony of John the Baptist, the apostle John describes Christ's first interactions with a select group of followers who would be His disciples. Jesus first met Peter and Andrew who happened to be disciples of John the

Baptist. They heard John declare that Jesus is "the Lamb of God, who takes away the sin of the world!" (1:29, 36) and started following Jesus. Then, Jesus meets Philip. The text doesn't indicate how this initial encounter with him took place. Jesus wasn't publically preaching yet, at least we have no record that He was. So the chance meeting was probably not from one of His amazing sermons. Maybe they bumped into each other in the market place. Perhaps they were at the same campfire or inn. Could it be that one of them joined the other while walking to Cana, where Jesus would perform His first miracle – changing water into wine (Jn. 2:1-12)? Might Peter and Andrew have been involved with the introductions? We don't know. All that is recorded is that Jesus "found Philip and said to him, 'Follow Me'" (Jn. 1:43).

Follow Me

This phrase, "Follow Me," was one of Jesus' calling cards. It was a way of inviting individuals to join His personal journey on earth and His Kingdom. Some time later, while walking along the Sea of Galilee, He again approached the two brothers, Peter and Andrew, and said, "Follow Me, and I will make you fishers of men" (Mt. 4:19). Immediately they left their nets and followed Him.[1]

Matthew, a tax collector, was sitting at his tax booth minding his own money-generating business when Christ called him to "follow Me." He got up, never to return to his former occupation. Rather, he immediately invited his former colleagues to meet with Jesus (Mt. 9:9–13).

Even non-disciples, those not part of the official twelve, were called to "follow Me." Jesus said, "If anyone would come after Me, let him deny himself and take up his cross and follow Me" (Mt. 16:24). To one rather self-righteous, rich young man who believed he had kept the law but was wondering what he still lacked, Jesus said, "If you would be perfect, go, sell what you possess and give to the poor, and you will have treasure in heaven; and come, follow Me" (Mt. 19:21).

This same message is given to us. Jesus said, "I am the way, and the truth, and the life. No one comes to the Father except through Me" (Jn. 14:6). We will not go to heaven unless we go through Jesus Christ. This requires following Him.

What Philip Didn't Know

Philip didn't know all that at this point. During the next three years, as he traversed the Holy Land with the Son of God, he would learn about Jesus, and after the resurrection of Christ, all of these truths and much more would become crystal clear.

At this time, all Philip had was a "brush with The Greatest," an encounter with someone he believed to be the One foretold by Moses and the prophets. Since his friend Nathanael was also looking for this One, or at least had studied about the prophesied One, Philip needed to tell him. But Philip did not have much knowledge about the Person he'd met. His rudimentary understanding of Jesus is evident in what he reported to Nathanael.

First, he called the Messiah "Jesus of Nazareth"[2] (Jn. 1:45). This was a true statement, but incomplete. Although Jesus grew up in Nazareth, He was born in Bethlehem. Anyone born elsewhere could not be the Messiah. The prophecy was clear: the Son of God would be born in Bethlehem, in the land of Judea (Mic. 5:2).[3]

This could be why Philip's friend Nathanael was a bit hesitant at first, asking: "Can anything good come out of Nazareth?" (Jn.1:46). Most conclude that he was a bit prejudiced toward those coming from this backwater, hick village. Could be. But perhaps he knew the Messiah was not to be from Nazareth.

Second, Philip identified the Messiah as "the son of Joseph" (Jn. 1:45). This was another popular way of distinguishing a person. Since the Jews did not have surnames at this time, they would use their father's name.[4] Biologically, however, Jesus was not from Joseph. In a legal sense He was related—Joseph was betrothed to Mary, the mother of Jesus. But Mary was a virgin when she conceived. According to the angel Gabriel, "The Holy Spirit will come upon you, and the power of the Most High will overshadow you" (Lk. 1:34-35). Jesus was not from the loins of Joseph; He was the Son of God. Speaking from a cloud during the transfiguration, God said: "This is My Son, My Chosen One, listen to Him!" (Lk. 9:35).

Philip's descriptions of Jesus showed that he didn't understand all the details about Jesus. But let's not be too critical. He had just met Jesus. The excitement of meeting the Savior of the world is often so overwhelming that we cannot contain ourselves or wait for more information. When we have the greatest "brush with Greatness," we have to tell others. This is repeated over and over as new believers, filled with excitement and anxious for their friends to have what they received, start sharing their faith.

Unfortunately, their limited knowledge and unbridled zeal can at times do more harm than good. Mistakes from this sudden fanaticism can initially turn off friends and relatives. That is why it is important to learn about evangelism—from personal study of God's Word, from godly pastors and teachers, and from books and courses on evangelism. If only the new believer's zeal could be repackaged and given to seasoned, mature believers who have lost their zeal, we'd have a winning combination. Instead, many believers are like the folks at the churches in Ephesus and Sardis, who abandoned their first love and had the reputation of being alive, but were dead (Rev. 2:5; 3:2). Christ exhorted them to wake up (3:2). May we, too, wake up. May the Lord restore our passion to see the lost come to a saving knowledge of Jesus Christ.

There is one more minor inaccuracy in what Philip told Nathanael. Philip said, "We have found Him" (Jn. 2:45). The *we* could be his friends Peter and Andrew, perhaps even John. But that's not the crux of the problem. Did Philip find Jesus, or did Jesus find him?

Let's be clear—neither from an experiential nor technical point did Philip or, for that matter, anyone, find the Messiah. In the text it is evident that Jesus found them (2:43). Even if people were brought to Him, as in the case of Nathanael, Jesus was still the one finding them. He continues to be the One to find people.

"No one can come to Me unless the Father who sent Me draws him," Jesus said (Jn. 6:44). "You did not choose Me, but I chose you and appointed you that you should go and bear fruit" (Jn. 15:16).[5]

This does not, however, diminish our role as soul-winners one iota. We are to follow the example of Philip and bring people to Jesus. We are the human agents God uses. It's encouraging to know that behind the scenes God is the One calling that person to Himself. We're not alone in this . . . not by a long shot.

Despite these minor miscues born out of such a short time with Jesus, God used Philip to bring his friend, Nathanael, to the Lord. And, it is believed, Nathanael became the disciple of Jesus known as Bartholomew.

The great 19th century English preacher, Charles Haddon Spurgeon, noted that we often witness out of ignorance. Our testimonies "are all imperfect, full of exaggerations of one truth, and misapprehensions of another." Fortunately, God still uses us, forgives our mistakes and blesses our ministries, never allowing His word to return void (Is. 55:11). In his sermon "Nathaniel and the Fig Tree," Spurgeon was quick to add, "We must try to avoid mistakes, lest we cause needless prejudice; we should so state the Gospel that if men are offended by it, it shall be the Gospel which offends them, and not our way of putting it."[6]

So, don't let your ignorance thwart your desire to witness or dampen your zeal. Learn as much as you can and witness anyway. God will work. Lives are depending on it.

The best Philip could do was to say to Nathanael's objections, "Come and see" (Jn. 2:46). That was enough to convince his friend to join him and come to Jesus. Basically when we witness to a lost soul that is what we are saying—come and see. Come and see for yourself the claims of Jesus Christ. The prophet Jeremiah wrote, "You will seek Me and find Me, when you seek for Me with all your heart" (Jer. 29:13). Likewise, Isaiah challenged us to "seek the LORD while He may be found; call upon Him while He is near" (Is. 55:6).

The Power of Friendship

What Philip did is the number one method of evangelism—one person who has had a spiritual life-altering experience telling another person, often a friend or relative, about Jesus Christ. Sure, other methods continue to have success: a Bible placed in a hotel room is opened by a weary and lonely traveler; a tract explaining the Good News is picked up in an unusual place; an evangelist proclaims the truth via the media or in a great crusade; a local pastor visits a dying man or woman in the hospital. These tactics and many more may introduce people to Jesus. (See the chapter "Tools for Sharing Your Faith," page 121, for further information.) But in most cases, it's a friend who is burdened about a lost friend and invites that friend to come and meet Jesus.

Might Philip have had the same success telling a complete stranger about having met Jesus? Perhaps, however, the testimony of a friend speaks volumes. There's an openness and trust which has been cultivated by years of interaction. A friend has earned the right to be heard and taken seriously. That was enough, despite Nathanael's initial reservation, to go and meet Jesus.

The success of friend-to-friend witnessing is evident in a statistic that, although a bit dated, stands the test of time. When researchers asked new converts, "What was the major influence in leading you to Christ and the Church?" a small percentage mentioned church advertising, the pastor or organized evangelism programs (2%, 6%, 6%, respectively). But a whopping 86 percent came to know Jesus Christ because of friends or relatives. An overwhelming majority point to the influence of their family and friends![7] A lot of money goes into other methods of sharing the Good News, and rightfully so. But an even greater emphasis should be placed on teaching friends how to reach out to their friends.

On a personal level, this should tell us that unsaved friends, relatives, coworkers, neighbors and classmates are dependent on us to shine the light of salvation so they can either receive or reject it. I don't mean to saddle you with guilt from a divine obligation that is being ignored—wait a minute, that's exactly what I intend to do. That's the purpose of this book. I not only want to convince you that you are God's chosen mouthpiece, but also give you the tools so that you can share your faith in a non-confrontational, loving manner with your friends.

This is called—"friendship," "lifestyle," or "relationship evangelism." I'm calling it "friend-to-friend" evangelism. It's simply sharing your faith with the people God has purposely placed in your life.

The Next Step

Over a Sunday lunch of soup and salad, the hostess asked me to explain "friendship evangelism." This caught me off guard. In the opening remarks before my sermon, I had mentioned the evangelism ministry in which I'm involved (800FollowMe.com) and our desire to put together an evangelism program for churches that would not only teach evangelism, but get the entire church involved. I thought everyone knew what friendship evangelism is—friends reaching friends. I don't remember my exact response to her, but I probably dodged the question moving quickly to explain the program we were designing. She followed up in a subsequent email. "My question to you was—what is the next step after you make friends?"

She hit the nail on the head. We don't make friends with non-believers so that we can boast of having non-believing friends. It is true that many believers (and my hand is raised on this one) have so cloistered themselves that the only friends they have are part of the Kingdom. So actually befriending a non-believer could be material for boasting. Or maybe you're a nice person and have lots of friends – saved and unsaved. That's not the purpose.

Nor is the purpose just to be a light hoping these non-believing friends will see our stellar Christian lifestyle, desire it, and ask how they can have it. This might happen if we are perfectly walking with the Lord—but who is? Vulnerability while making friends can be messy and will often show kinks in the armor and carnal blemishes—the old nature. How many of us can keep our light shining perfectly bright all the time without fail? Further, will our unbelieving friend ever really put two and two together, equating our "niceness" to our Christian faith and thus desiring it?

Is it evangelism if there are no words? That's the question Scot McKnight asked in his blog, *Jesus Creed*. He was quick to cite what the Apostle Paul wrote in Romans 10: "But how are they to call on Him in whom they have not believed? And how are they to believe in Him of whom they have never heard?" (vs.14). A verbalization needs to take place along with the witness of our life. McKnight writes: "The ineradicable form of evangelism is to declare the story of Jesus. All other dimensions gain their only clarity once that declaration is clear."[8]

My hostess friend wrote: "Certainly, I am ready and willing to share my testimony with any friend who asks me. The problem is no one is asking. It may take more time for people to see a difference in our lives and wonder why." Yes, it may—and it may never happen. Our friends may never ask about the hope within us. Therefore, evangelism has to be more than just walking-the-walk. We have to talk-the-talk! We need to become intentional with our witnessing.

Making friends with non-believers so that we can invite them to a church where they will hear the Gospel or will be corralled by the pastor or elders and shown the way is not a bad idea. Inviting non-believers to church is a great way to expose them to Christ, especially if the church is actively seeking those who are lost. But this book is more concerned with the responsibility to evangelize that lies within each of us. You, me, we are to go and make disciples (Mt. 28:19). The commission has been given to us. Naturally, I will suggest that you invite your friends to

Christian activities, but shouldn't you be able to share your faith? I know, I know—it is difficult to do, and we are afraid. But we can do this, and we must.

An Eternal Priority

The priority of friend-to-friend evangelism is evident when you recognize that your unbelieving friends, if they die in this condition, will spend eternity separated from God. They will die and go to Hell. Some suggest Jesus spoke more about Hell than He did about Heaven. I'm not sure that is verifiable, but His goal was to prevent people from going there. "I have come that they may have life" (Jn. 10:10). "Whoever believes in Him is not condemned, but whoever does not believe is condemned already, because he has not believed in the name of the only Son of God" (Jn. 3:18). "Depart from Me, you cursed, into the eternal fire prepared for the devil and his angels" (Mt. 25:41).

As followers of Jesus Christ, we should be driven by the fact that our loved ones and friends who do not know Christ will spend a Christ-less eternity. Spurgeon wrote: "If sinners be damned, at least let them leap to Hell over our dead bodies. And if they perish, let them perish with our arms wrapped about their knees, imploring them to stay. If Hell must be filled, let it be filled in the teeth of our exertions, and let not one go unwarned and unprayed for."[9] Certainly not our friends!

We might be the only Jesus our friends ever see. God may have purposely placed them in our lives at this time so that we will share the Good News of Jesus. I'm a firm believer God is the One who saves and all those He calls will be saved (Eph. 1:4), but this truth does not diminish our role or relieve us from these evangelistic duties. Jesus has left us as His witnesses on earth (Acts 1:8). He has commanded us to go and make disciples (Mt. 28:19). Nor should we cushion the mandate by softening the stark warnings about Hell. Spurgeon's high view of God's sovereignty did not diminish his "shock treatment" to motivate Christians to share their faith.

If you were to list all your friends and family into two columns – those saved and those not saved – realizing the second group will spend eternity in Hell, might that not cause you to pray fervently for their souls and motivate you to share the Good News? Your friends and family members ARE your divine appointments.

In the words of David Platt – "What if God has placed every one of us in different locations with different jobs and different gifts around different people for the distinct purpose of every single one of us making disciples and multiplying churches? What if any follower of Christ could do this? What if every follower of Christ should do this?"[10] Every follower of Christ MUST!

Assuming we've had a brush with the Greatest, then we have been given the opportunity to share with our friends, relatives, co-workers and others the greatest story ever told, about the greatest offer ever made, by the greatest person who ever lived—Jesus Christ. What a privilege to be assigned this task by the God who created all things, saved us, and now commissions us!

We start like Philip with a desire to bring our friend to meet Christ by sharing the Gospel. So, what is the Gospel?

For Further Thought:

1. Ask a friend or prospective relationship for three things you could pray about for them, and then check back with them in the future.
2. Try to resolve a broken relationship with a friend. Admit you were wrong and ask forgiveness.
3. Ask your friends (acquaintances, new contacts, everyone) *truthfully*, "How are you?" before jumping into your agenda. See what doors open to your genuine heart for them.
4. Do you view those in your daily encounters as possible relationships for many years to come, possibly eternally?
5. Who is your Nathanael? _____

2

Stumped on the Gospel ... No More!
What's the Fuss?
Acts 8:26-40

The Gospel. The Gospel. What is the Gospel of Jesus Christ? This is what stumped a government official from Ethiopia while he was sitting in a chariot in the desert and reading a passage from Isaiah 53. The text didn't use the term *Gospel*, but it describes the Gospel. Soon he would understand. Enter Phillip.

This is not the same Philip from the previous chapter, the disciple of Jesus Christ. This Philip, a Greek convert, is a disciple, for sure, but he enters the picture a bit later.

Jesus had died and risen from the grave. He had appeared to His followers over the course of 40 days and then ascended into Heaven. The disciples, who soon would be called "apostles" (meaning "a messenger of God"), followed the Lord's instructions to stay in Jerusalem until they were filled with the Holy Spirit (Lk. 24:49; Acts 1:4,8). This happened on the Day of Pentecost. Three thousand people were saved that day, and others were added daily (Acts 2:41,47). The disciples, however, continued to cloister themselves in Jerusalem. This was all new to them. Going beyond the city limits was a scary proposition, not to mention the fact they were riding the crest of great success within the city. It wasn't until persecution came busting down the doors, forcing them to flee the city, that they began to fulfill

Christ's commission, their world-wide evangelistic outreach.

The Philip of this chapter is first mentioned in Acts 6 when "seven men of good repute, full of the Spirit and of wisdom" (vs. 3) were selected to serve the needs of widows, thus allowing the apostles to devote themselves to prayer and the ministry of the Word (vs. 4). The elementary job descriptions of deacons and apostles indicates this Philip was not one of the Twelve. Philip, the apostle, would have been doing "apostle" work, not "deacon" work. Not that either is wrong; both are definitely needed.

Persecution and Preaching

Before long, two of the seven rose in reputation because of their capacity for preaching and performing signs and wonders. Stephen, who was mentioned first of the seven, was brought before the Jewish council on charges of "blasphemous words against Moses and God" (vs. 11). He blew them away with his knowledge of Jewish history and running commentary on God's dealings with the Jews leading up to, and including, "the Righteous One [Jesus Christ], whom you have now betrayed and murdered" (7:52). So forceful and factual was his indictment against them they "ground their teeth at him" (vs. 54). There may have been some snarling and snorting going on as well. Then they "cried out with a loud voice, stopped their ears" (vss. 54, 57) and dragged him outside the city, stoning him to death.[1]

Our Philip evades the ensuing persecution by leaving Jerusalem and going into the area of Samaria to preach. "Now those who were scattered went about preaching the word. Philip went down to the city of Samaria and proclaimed to them the Christ" (Acts 8:4-5).

You will recall, much to the chagrin of the disciples, Jesus also went into Samaritan territory and witnessed to a woman whom He met at a well (Jn. 4). The Jews despised Samaritans. They were half-breeds—half Jewish and half Gentile. In fact, Jews would travel many miles to go around Samaria to avoid potential contact. So for Philip to go to the Samaritans to spread the Gospel was not only groundbreaking in race relations, but was setting the tone for Christianity. The Kingdom of God was not to be limited to Jews. As the child's song goes, "Red, brown, yellow, black and white, all are precious in His sight; Jesus loves the little children of the world."

Much Joy

Philip was having great success preaching the "good news about the kingdom of God and the name of Jesus Christ" in Samaria (Acts 8:12). Unclean spirits were cast out of those who were possessed. Many were healed, including those who were paralyzed or lame (vs. 7). And many were being baptized. There was much joy in that city (8:8).

Truer words have never been spoken. When Jesus enters the life of a person, there is not only rejoicing in Heaven (Lk. 15:10), there is great joy among new and old believers. Just think how happy you will be when your Nathanael (friend, son or daughter, parent, co-worker, or neighbor) comes to a saving knowledge of Jesus Christ.

Chuck and I would go to a fast food place to have an apple dumpling with chocolate ice cream every time someone received the Lord during one of our *Evangelism Explosion* outings. On one occasion, a follow-up visit with a young woman who had put her faith in Jesus Christ, we found her entire family visiting her. Not wanting to intrude on this family time, we politely attempted to take leave with the hopes of coming back another time. We were stopped in our tracks when her mother announced, "Something happened to my daughter. She's different. I want to know about it." We immediately went into the trailer and soon saw God's saving grace fall on that entire family. I don't think Chuck and I shared the dumpling and ice cream that night. We each had our own! It was our little way of celebrating. There are plenty of other ways with less calories to celebrate. All I know is there is great rejoicing when those who were spiritually blind receive their sight.

Into the Desert

Back to our story about Philip ... When the apostles heard what was happening in Samaria, they sent Peter and John to help. As these two leaders of the Apostles prayed for the new converts, the Samaritans received the Spirit just as the Jewish believers had (8:17)—thus verifying that they were equal members in the Kingdom. On their way back to Jerusalem, Peter and John continued their preaching to the Samaritans. Philip, however, was sent by the Lord into the desert—"to the road that goes down from Jerusalem to Gaza (8:26). He happened upon a chariot in which "there was an Ethiopian, a eunuch, a court official of Candace, queen of the Ethiopians, who was in charge of all her treasure" (vs. 27).[2]

Luke, the writer of Acts, identifies this fellow in precise terms. First, his nationality—Ethiopian. This term could refer to anyone from Africa with dark skin. But here he appears to be identified with the queen, Candace, from the ancient kingdom of Meroe, which was located in northern Sudan. Candace was a title, like "Queen Mother, ruling monarch."[3]

Second, his condition—eunuch. A eunuch was a castrated man. This often happened early in life and without one's consent. It was hoped a eunuch would be a loyal and reliable servant. The term originally meant "guard of the bedchamber or harem." People must have figured he would be no threat to the girls. But that was not the post of this man. He was a court official, treasurer of the queen. He was a very important person who had risen to a trusted governmental office.

Third, the reason for him being in Jerusalem—to worship. We can only assume he was a proselyte to Judaism. This could be why the disciples did not have a problem with this Gentile becoming a believer. He was already a practicing Jew.

Finally, the eunuch was headed back to Ethiopia. While reading the Scriptures, he got stuck on a prophecy from Isaiah. "Do you understand what you are reading?" Philip asked the man (8:30). "How can I, unless someone guides me?" was the response (vs. 31).

The prophet Isaiah, in Isaiah 53, was talking about the coming Messiah. "Like a lamb that is led to slaughter, and like a sheep that before its shearers is silent, so He opened not His mouth" (Is. 53:7). The Ethiopian was stumped. "About whom does the prophet say this, about himself or about someone else?" (Acts 8:34).

If ever there was a softball question, a divinely inspired opening, this was it. Philip knew exactly what to say, "and beginning with this Scripture he told him the good news about Jesus" (vs. 35).

To finish the story, the man believed and, upon coming to some water, was baptized. Philip, then, miraculously disappeared and found himself at Azotus thirty miles away. We're talking the Star Trek transporter without the teleportation machine and no "Beam me up, Scotty." One moment Philip was here and the next, after rematerialization (or something), there. No smoke and mirrors or clever cinematography, it was God moving him in an instant. If only we could travel to other countries this way. No more "multi-day" treks in and out of airports, not being able to stretch my legs, with the drone of the airplane tormenting me as it is now on this 14-hour flight from New Delhi to New York ... but I digress.

From Azotus, also known as Ashdod, Philip continued to preach at every town heading north along the coast of the Mediterranean Sea until he reached Caesarea (vs. 40). He apparently spent many years there (Acts 21:8).

And the Ethiopian, what happened to him? We don't know for sure. Church Father Irenaeus, Bishop of Lyons, more than a century later, wrote that this man, who was supposedly named Simeon Bachos, went throughout Ethiopia preaching the Good News. Perhaps he played a role in the start of, or at least setting the groundwork for, the Ethiopian church. By the fourth century, Christianity was the state religion of Ethiopia.[4]

The Message

So what was it Philip preached to the Samaritans, the Ethiopian, and from city to city? The Gospel.

"The Gospel. The Gospel. What is the Gospel of Jesus Christ?" The sound of popular preacher and author John Piper, from Desiring God Ministries, rings in my ears with this question and his subsequent answer. "The Gospel is the Good News that Jesus Christ, the Righteous One, died for our sins and rose again, eternally triumphant over all His enemies. So there is now no condemnation for those who believe, but only everlasting joy." [5]

Piper is referencing First Corinthians 15:1-4. These are the verses my preacher dad told me to learn for my ordination council. When he quizzed me about the Gospel I must have given him a sloppy answer. To which he said, "Danny, they are going to ask you what the Gospel is. Know these verses." As an aside, he also gave me a hint as to how to survive the ordination ordeal. He told me to think of a few theological conundrums and controversial issues that might cause the guys to debate among themselves. This is similar to what the Apostle Paul did before the Sanhedrin when he announced his belief in the resurrection pitting the Pharisees against the Sadducees (Acts 23). Both pieces of advice worked perfectly.

In order for us to go to our friends and present the hope that is within us, we need to have a clear understanding of what the Gospel, the Good News, is.

But why? Why do we need to know the Gospel?

First, it is God's plan for us. Jesus' death was no accident. The Apostle Paul noted it was "according to the will of our God and Father" (Gal. 1:4). Peter said Jesus was "delivered up according to the definite plan and foreknowledge of God" and adds "God foretold by the mouth of all the prophets, that his Christ would suffer" (Acts 2:23; 3:18). God's plan, by which we may be saved, is contained in the Gospel of Jesus Christ. Thus, its importance cannot be overstated.

Moreover, there is only one Gospel. There are not two or three Gospels. There's not one Gospel for you and one for me or for different people groups. How cruel would God be to have His "only begotten Son" put to death if there was another way to get to Heaven? There is only one. The church in Galatia was in danger of turning to another gospel. It was contrary to what God revealed. Paul wrote this church to let them know he didn't invent the Gospel. He didn't even learn it from others. God gave it to him (Gal. 1:6-12). The fact that there is one Gospel is important. It means we have not followed fables of men (2 Pet. 1:16). And it means there are serious consequences for preaching another gospel.

So what is the Gospel? First and foremost it centers on Jesus Christ and what He did for us. Jesus, God's Son, did not come into this world just to teach good, moral and upright standards of living. He did not come solely for the purpose of performing miracles, even though He healed the sick, gave sight to the blind, cast out demons, and even brought some dead people back to life. He was not on the earth to start a revolution, nor was He here to show the hypocrisy of the Jewish religion and how it had become bloated with laws and was out of touch with what God intended.

Jesus, God's Son, the Messiah, came to die for the sins of the world. His death was not, as the author of *Killing Jesus* proposed, over a money issue from upsetting the money changers in the Temple. Money may have been a motivating factor for putting Jesus to death along with the fear of losing their power and having Rome take more control. The true causes ran deeper and were spiritual. The Chief Priests and religious establishment wanted Jesus dead because, according to them, He was breaking the Sabbath and "He was even calling God His own Father, making Himself equal with God" (Jn 5:18). He claimed to be the Messiah and thus, God. This claim challenged their authority and, it appeared, was about to upset the fig cart. Mistakenly, they thought eliminating Jesus would put an end to what they considered to be damaging tomfoolery. Boy, were they wrong!

Stumped on the Gospel ... No More!

Jesus said, "I came that they may have life and have it more abundantly" (Jn. 10:10). In order to do that, the Good Shepherd needed to lay down His life for His sheep (vs. 11). Why? Why did Jesus need to die?

God created humans sinless with the opportunity to remain that way or to rebel. Remember the forbidden tree in the Garden of Eden? God told Adam and Eve they could have anything in the Garden they wanted, but "of the tree of the knowledge of good and evil you shall not eat," (Gen. 2:16-17). This was a test of their obedience. From our present, fallen condition, some might label it an unfair test, because we all know if a park bench has a "Wet Paint" sign on it, we are driven to touch the bench. When we are told "no," we immediately attempt to do it or start contriving ways to get around the "no." I saw this with my children and now my grandchildren. I see it in myself. It's in our fallen nature. We don't need to be taught this. Adam and Eve, however, were created innocent without that inner urge to rebel. Nevertheless they sinned against God by disobeying and eating of that tree.

Because of their sin, we are all sinners. "Therefore, just as sin came into the world through one man, and death through sin, and so death spread to all men because all sinned" (Rom. 5:12).

Adam and Eve did not die physically, right away, but they did die spiritually.[6] Their spiritual death immediately separated them from God and this would lead to an eternal separation. "For the wages of sin is death" (Rom. 6:23). Same goes for us.

But wait—God had a plan. Oh, am I thankful He had a plan! We'd be eternally doomed without it. His plan sent His only begotten Son, Jesus Christ, the sinless One, to come into the world as a human and become the perfect sacrifice for sin—the only sacrifice God could accept. Prior to Christ's coming, the righteous followers of God would bring animal sacrifices to the Tabernacle or Temple. God accepted this form of sacrifice, this shedding of blood, but, it was a foreshadowing or prequel to the ultimate sacrifice by His Son. The writer of Hebrews wrote, "Indeed, under the law almost everything is purified with blood, and without the shedding of blood there is no forgiveness of sin"

(Heb. 9:22).

So God's plan had Jesus sacrificially dying on the cross for our sins. It is called a gift: "For God so loved the world that He gave His only begotten Son, that whosoever believeth in Him, should not perish but have everlasting life" (Jn. 3:16, KJV). This gift is offered to all who believe.

Only One Way

The first point of the Gospel centers on Jesus Christ and what He did for us. The second point is the part we play. It doesn't happen unless God begins a work in us, but there obviously is a human element. This is where belief comes in. We need to believe the Gospel, the Good News. Back to Piper, we need to believe "that Jesus Christ, the Righteous One, died for our sins and rose again, eternally triumphant over all His enemies. So there is now no condemnation for those who believe, but only everlasting joy. That's the Gospel."

But aren't there many ways in which a person can get to Heaven?

Most people in the world today assume there is more than one path to eternal bliss. They advocate "all roads (or religions) lead to Heaven." Since most attempt to place God within their human perspective, their own box, and define Him on their terms, they conclude that this "God of love" does not want anyone to be separated from Him and, therefore, He has made many paths to reach Him. They teach that one can believe in the God of the Bible, the god of Islam, the many gods of Hinduism, or no god at all, and still get to Heaven. This could not be further from the truth! Jesus definitively and distinctly declared, "I am the way, the truth, and the life. No one comes to the Father except through Me" (Jn. 14:6).

As has been noted by many but popularized by C. S. Lewis in his book *Mere Christianity*, Jesus' statement proves that He is either a liar, a lunatic or the Lord. Obviously, we believe He is Lord, and His statement is Gospel truth. There is no other path to meet God. If we wish to go to Heaven when we die, we must go through Jesus Christ.

Another lie of the Evil One is—we can make it on our own terms or through our own religion. In most religions, as Tim Keller has noted, their gods reveal what one must do in order to reach them—from denying an assortment of things, to performing various sacred tasks, to giving large amounts of money. But the God of the Bible achieved salvation for us through His only begotten Son. We cannot achieve salvation. We cannot do enough. We cannot erase our sin. Only the sinless One, Jesus Christ, can do this.

So, how does one get saved?

Salvation comes by receiving the gift God presents to us. "For by grace you have been saved through faith. And this is not your own doing; it is the gift of God, not a result of works, so that no one may boast" (Eph. 2:8-9). It's no more complicated than that. This is why a child can believe and why Jesus praised childlike faith (Mt. 18:3). God offers us the gift of eternal life. All we need to do is receive that gift. This is where faith and repentance fit in.

What is faith?

Let's start with what it is not. Many place their faith or trust in good works. Others think they're not really that bad of a person. If their works were placed on scales, the good would definitely outweigh the bad. Certainly, they're not as wicked as mass murderers, serial killers, rapists and the like. Others would attribute their faith to their family, church, or religion. They faithfully attend services and observe whatever rules and regulations are set before them. Some suggest they've been baptized, maybe as a baby, and therefore are "in." Yet, as one Southern preacher used to say, "It doesn't matter if you've been baptized so many times every fish in the ocean knows you by your first name." It's not works. It's not family. It's not religion. It's not baptism. It's not confirmation. It's not our goodness outweighing wickedness. It's not even our good looks.

Stumped on the Gospel ... No More!

My favorite definition of faith comes from the *Evangelism Explosion* program popularized by the late D. James Kennedy: "Faith is trusting in Christ alone for your salvation." It is Jesus – alone! As the late Jerry Falwell used to say, "It is faith in Christ alone – plus nothing, minus nothing!" And faith is a gift God gives to us as His Holy Spirit works in our life. Only through Jesus Christ can we have salvation.

Where does repentance fit in?

Repentance is a part of faith. It is not separate from faith or added to it. Repentance and faith are two sides of the same coin.

Repentance is the natural expression of our faith. As we recognize our separation from God because of sin, we realize our sin is why Jesus died on the cross – to pay the penalty for our sin, the sin that would have kept us separated from God for all eternity. We should respond with godly sorrow when this truth finally hits us—"He died for me and my sin!" Acknowledging the truth of our sin and turning from it is to repent (Acts 11:18; 20:21; 2 Tim. 2:25; 2 Pet. 3:9).[7]

Unless We Speak

So when Philip spoke to the Ethiopian official, he explained that the Prophet Isaiah was writing about Jesus. And then he shared the Gospel, the Good News.

I'm not sure how often you will have softball questions like the Ethiopian's or a divinely inspired opening so obvious. However, when you are speaking to your friends about the hope that is within you, you need to make sure you know the Gospel of Jesus Christ and are able to explain it.

The question from the Ethiopian burns within me. When Philip inquired if he understood what he was reading, he asked: "How can I, unless someone guides me?" (Acts 8:31).

How can your friends and family, your Nathanael, know about Jesus Christ and what He did on the cross—the Gospel, the Good News—unless you tell them? They may look up into a starlit sky and acknowledge there must be something more than a big bang theory to explain it. There must be a Being that is beyond and behind all of this. They may observe the intricacies of nature, the birth of a child, the diversity of the animal kingdom, and finally come to the place where evolution's explanation doesn't cut it or make sense. There must be someone who designed all of this. But how will they know Who that Someone is if you don't tell them?

The Apostle Paul's words reverberate down through the centuries: "How are they to call on Him in whom they have not believed? And how are they to believe in Him of whom they have never heard?" (Rom. 10:14).

The task of sharing the Gospel falls on us!

Core Truths

So what is the Gospel? Let's summarize:

1. We are all sinners and cannot save ourselves.
2. Because of this, we are and will be separated from God for all eternity.
3. The only "saving grace" is that God sent His perfect Son, totally divine and totally human, to come into this world and pay the ransom for us by suffering the punishment we sinners deserve. This required dying on the cross for our sins.
4. Jesus not only did this, but He rose again, conquering death. He appeared to many over forty days.[8] He went into Heaven and is coming back in judgment.
5. All those who by faith repent of their sins and trust Christ alone for their salvation are born again into a new life, an eternal life in Christ.

Now that you have heard the Gospel, the Good News about Jesus Christ, have you repented of your sins and trusted in Christ alone for your salvation? Borrowing again from D. James Kennedy's *Evangelism Explosion*: "If you were to die today, are you sure you'd go to Heaven? And suppose you were to die and stand before God and He were to ask you why He should let you into Heaven, what would your answer be?"

If your answer has anything to do with religion, family upbringing, your works and what you've done, or your good looks, then it's an eternally damning answer that will keep you separated from God. No second chances after death. Salvation comes by faith, repenting of your sins and trusting in Christ alone. If you have not done that, you can right now. You can do it by simply praying to Jesus and receiving Him as your Savior. "But to all who did receive Him, who believed in His name, He gave the right to become children of God" (Jn. 1:12).

Church evangelist Wendell Calder has a short prayer he often uses at the end of salvation sermons. There's nothing particularly sacred about the words. They're not magical. Saying the words of this prayer will not save you even if you were to say them every day for the next 100 years. It's not the words that save. However, if by faith you desire to receive the gift of eternal life, this prayer or one like it, from your heart, could express that desire.

Dear Lord Jesus, I admit to You that I am a sinner. I have failed You and deserve Your judgment. Thank you, Jesus, for dying on the cross for me and my sin and rising from the dead.

Dear Lord Jesus, right now I call upon You to come into my life, forgive my sin and save me. In Jesus' Name I pray. Amen.

Being assured of your salvation is the first step in actually sharing your faith. What are some of the other steps?

For Further Thought:

1. How many people have you heard, in regards to their certainty of heaven, use the words, "I hope . . ."?
2. If you were undertaking a mini-ordination, could you boldly

articulate the gospel? If yes, how?
3. Do you see yourself equipped as a message-giver carrying a crucial message?
4. Would you alert others if they were in imminent danger? How about to life and life abundantly?
5. Are you continuing to pray for your Nathanael?

3

The Correct Source
Where Power Lies
Acts 19:11-20

R alph, Mike, Richard, Henry, George, Forrest and Arnold—
okay, those weren't their names. They probably had Jewish
names with, perhaps, a Roman flair. They were seven sons of
a Jewish high priest, Sceva, who lived in Ephesus, and they all
got beat up by one man (Acts 19:11-16).

This was not from a witnessing experience. No worries there.
Rather, they were trying to exorcize a demon. And they failed,
miserably. Headlines in the *Ephesus Express* the next morning:
"Raving Maniac Overpowers Seven Brothers."

Demon Trouble

Demon possession is mentioned numerous times in the New
Testament. Often Jesus encountered possessed people who acted
out with epileptic seizures, the inability to speak or hear,
blindness, or other abnormalities. On one occasion, Jesus
happened upon a man on the east coast of the Sea of Galilee who
was possessed with a large number of demons. A "legion" they
called themselves (Lk. 8:26-39). This man, who lived naked
among tombstones, had superhuman strength like the one in
Ephesus. "He was kept under guard and bound with chains and
shackles, but he would break the bonds and be driven by the
demon into the desert" (vs. 29). When Jesus cast out the demons,

they went into a herd of pigs which fled down a hillside into the drink, drowning themselves, but leaving the man in his right mind. He desired to follow Jesus, but Jesus told him, "Return to your home, and declare how much God has done for you" (vs. 39). The man became a great witness for Jesus.

This is what soul-winning is all about. Soul-winning is just going to your family, your friends, and acquaintances, and telling them what God through Jesus Christ has done for you. It is no more complicated than that.

I'm a huge fan of organized witnessing programs especially *Evangelism Explosion* which was featured at my church for years. Many learned how to share their faith, a good number received the Lord, and the church grew. The church of a pastor buddy of mine uses *The Way of the Master*. There are other equally good programs that develop a witnessing core who can go out from a church to capture their town for Christ. Not everyone has the advantage of such an organization or a church that is able to pull this off. But everyone—every Christian—can do exactly what this man did—tell their friends what God did for them. May this formerly demon-possessed man be an example for us.

In our day, especially in the West, demonic activity is not considered by physical or mental health professionals. Nor will you see coverage for "demon possession" in health insurance plans. It is a problem in other countries, especially India. One New Delhi pastor friend, Vijay, says the reason is that Hindus have so many false gods. In their idolatry, they have given themselves over to the Evil One. In the West, many characteristics of demon possession receive other explanations: mental illness, seizures, depression. Such conditions may not be induced by anything demonic. Then again, they might. I'm convinced when all is said and done and revealed in Heaven, we're going to learn there was a lot more demonic influence than we realized. The Hitlers of the world were either possessed or greatly influenced by the Evil One and his horde of demons.

The man in Ephesus was so possessed that he had enough superhuman strength to beat up seven men. I like to say I have the strength of ten men. Back in the day this was no idle boast. Even now, if I were teamed up with six other guys, all of us could "put a hurtin" on one man. But this man, while possessed, was like Samson or Rambo.

Before the demon-possessed man put a hurting on them, he made an interesting observation: "Jesus I know, and Paul I recognize, but who are you?" (Acts 19:15).

The Power We Need

The entire story comes on the heels of God's great work in the city of Ephesus. At first, the Apostle Paul discovered some righteous people in town who had been baptized into John the Baptist's baptism. Paul acknowledged that John's baptism, although good in regards to repentance, was not for salvation. "John baptized with the baptism of repentance, telling the people to believe in the One who was to come after him, that is, Jesus" (19:4). Salvation comes through faith in Jesus. When these folks became believers in Jesus Christ, they were baptized into Him and a church was established.

Aquila and Priscilla, who had accompanied Paul from Corinth and were fellow tentmakers, became charter members of the church. Before Paul left, as a result of a riot and major uproar that was a reaction to Paul's ministry, he saw great success with all sorts of "extraordinary miracles . . . so that even handkerchiefs or aprons that had touched his skin were carried away to the sick, and their diseases left them and the evil spirits came out of them" (vs.11-12). This spurred on others who thought they could conjure up, through human means, the same type of power (similar to false preachers today). Enter the seven sons of Sceva.

The power of God is not something that can be manipulated.

Another example is Simon the magician in Samaria. Simon was so impressed with the power of Peter and John to impart the Holy Spirit he offered the disciples a bribe so he could do the same (Acts 8:14-19). He was soundly rebuked and, some believe, he genuinely repented. At least he asked for prayer (vs. 24). His story shows that it is God's power that saves people.

We cannot evangelize in our own power; we must depend on God's power. There are several ways we can do this. We will explore some of these in the chapter to follow. In this chapter, I'd like to examine one area – the inward life of a soul-winner.

The Spirit Within

Indwelling every believer is the Holy Spirit. He enters at conversion (Rom. 8:9), which is why a Christian cannot be possessed by a demon. Since the Holy Spirit has taken up residence there's no room for the archenemy (2 Cor. 1:22; 5:5; 1 Cor. 6:19; Mark 3:24-26). Unfortunately, many Christians are not yielded to the Holy Spirit. The tendency is to stray from the things of God and cling to this world, which we are commanded not to do (Rom. 12:1). Granted, we have to be in the world, but the world should not be in us. This is easier said than done.

Many Christians experience what's called the roller-coaster life. Sometimes they are up, walking with God, feeling great, faithfully attending church, in their Bibles on a regular basis, even sharing their faith with their friends. Other times, unfortunately, they are in the depths of despair. Lower than low. Bottomed-out. Hiding from any opportunity to share Christ. Certainly not "ready in season and out of season" (2 Tim. 4:2).

Sin is generally the root cause of this problem. As they give in to the Evil One, their own selfish desires, and the world – "the desires of the flesh, the desires of the eyes, and pride in possessions" (1 Jn. 2:16), they seem to move further and further from God and the victorious Christian life. The Holy Spirit is still there. God promised never to leave us or forsake us (Heb. 13:5b). But they are not yielded to God.

This descent may not happen rapidly. It is often a gradual thing. As newborn babes in Christ, believers are very excited about their newfound faith. They cannot get enough of God. Sins that held them captive are addressed and dealt with. They start to grow in the Lord. But then gradually they hit a few speed bumps and – Bam! – right into some walls. The enticements of the flesh and all the things of this world take a toll, and believers tend to fall back into practices long since gone. As far as witnessing goes—they'd have a very hard time telling how much God has done for them (Luke 8:39).

Then there are other believers who are more subdued in their Christian life. They initially bought into "fire insurance" and believe they are on their way to Heaven, but that's about it. They remain like babies all their life. Sin may not rule in an overt fashion, but the fact they are not growing is a sign of either not being a true follower of Jesus or they are unyielded to Him. These people cannot tell how much God has done for them, because either they don't remember what He has done or don't know how to explain it. And, tragically, they are unwilling to learn.

Both are in need of revival. Their spirits need to be revived so that they can become excited about telling others, especially their friends, about their faith.

True Obedience

There are various things we could address at this point, but let's look at one. The inward life of a soul-winner requires obedience to God. Jesus is the prime example. He was always, without fail, obedient to the Father: "Nevertheless, not My will, but Yours, be done" (Lk. 22:42). Christ's entire life and ministry were orchestrated by His Father, and Jesus did everything His Father wanted Him to do. Even His coming to the earth was a fulfillment of God's will and desire. This was the plan of the ages. This was how God would restore men to Himself. Christ had to be obedient to the Father for God's plan of salvation to work.

Could you imagine if Jesus decided maybe He'd slack off on a few things? Perhaps eating a little bread when He was supposed to be fasting wouldn't be such a bad idea, especially if it was hot-out-of-the-oven. Maybe jumping off a high place to be rescued by angels who would attend to His needs might be exhilarating, like bungee jumping. Or how about immediately becoming the king of the world with all the power, success and adulation that accompanies it (Mt. 4:1-11)? If Christ had done any of these things or less, in direct disobedience to His Father, we'd be doomed. He had to be one hundred percent obedient, completely sinless in order to be that perfect sacrifice (Heb. 4:15; 7:26)

Followers of Jesus and soul-winners must have this same type of obedience. Not perfect, but striving for holiness.

What is obedience and what does it mean to be obedient to God?

The following definition, learned in college, was so good we used it for our children. "Obedience is doing exactly what you are told to do, immediately, with the right heart attitude." This means not deviating from what you are to do. Not doing your own thing, but doing "exactly" what you were instructed. Not waiting until it is convenient or on your own time schedule, but doing it "immediately." And having the "right heart attitude" while you are doing it – not begrudgingly, but willingly and cheerfully.

The same factors fit our obedience to God. We need to do what He tells us to do. We should do it right away. And we should do it out of a loving heart. From the Biblical standpoint, this means to hear, to trust, to submit, to surrender to God, and to obey His Word.

In what areas should we be obedient?

Lee Andrew Henderson identifies six areas of obedience mentioned in Scriptures.[1] The first four are often listed together concerning our love. We should love and obey God with all our heart, all our will, all our mind, and all our strength (Mk. 12:30). The heart is the core of our being. This must be totally devoted to God. Our will needs to conform to God's will. Our mind, which often becomes the devil's workshop, needs to be submitted to Him. And our strength needs to be consecrated to God for His purposes, not our selfish desires.

Henderson adds two more areas of obedience – our finances and future. Both are areas in which we attempt to maintain control, but tend to struggle. We must be obedient to God in these areas as well. Jesus said, "If you love Me, you will keep My commandments" (Jn. 14:15).

We must contribute one more to this list. How could we leave witnessing and evangelizing out of a book on personal evangelism? Commands are very clear on this point. "Go, therefore and make disciples" (Mt. 28:19), Jesus commanded. Jesus stated - "You shall be My witnesses" (Acts 1:8). To not be a witness for Jesus Christ is to be disobedient to God.

To the children of Israel Moses wrote, "The whole commandment that I command you today you shall be careful to do that you may live and multiply" (Dt. 8:1). Obedience to God results in blessings from God. The key characteristic of all thriving Christians is their obedience to God.

Obedience begins, then, with a willingness to follow Christ, and that's no small order. "If any would come after me," Jesus said, "let him deny himself, take up his cross daily and follow Me" (Lk. 9:23). To "deny oneself" means to renounce the right to rule yourself. This is total submission to God—to let Him rule you. Don't let this scare you. He's never failed one person yet. "Whoever loses His life for My sake, will save it" (vs. 24).

Next, Jesus said believers need to "take up their cross." This is not speaking about wearing cross figurines as jewelry. Nor is it referencing the "crosses we must all bear" – the common trials of life, such as annoying roommates, red lights, traffic, nagging spouses, to name a few. It's not even, as John MacArthur clarified, some mystical level of selfless "deeper spiritual life" that only the religious elite can hope to achieve.[2] Cross-bearing means to live like dead people—dead to ourselves and the world so that we can serve Christ. We are willing to pay any price for the cause of Christ.

Then we are to follow Christ. Here's that obedience a Christian must have. To follow Christ is to take Him for our Master, our Teacher, our Example. It is to believe what He taught, to uphold His cause, to obey His precepts, and to do it though it leads to Heaven by way of the cross.[3]

Off the Roller Coaster

Unfortunately, many Christians do not even try to follow Christ. Or after a while, they take themselves off the cross and decide to live their own lives. I hate to admit it, but I tend to do this. If that is you as well, we're in good company. The Apostle Paul struggled often doing the very things he should not do and not doing what he should (Rom. 7:15).

How can we have success in the Christian life and get off the roller coaster so that God will use us to win our friends to Christ?

Simply stated, we need to spend time with God. And the more we do, the more we will be like Him.

During a conference at Word of Life in Scroon Lake, NY, preacher and author Ray Pritchard called this the "doctrine of unconscious influence." The more time we spend with God, the more we will reflect His glory. Pritchard cites the story of Moses coming off the mountain after having spent days with God. Not only did Moses receive the Ten Commandments, he had a special opportunity to see God. No, he didn't see Him face to face. No man has seen God and lived (Ex. 33:20). But upon his request to see God, God placed him in the cleft of a rock and covered his eyes until His glory passed. Moses was given a once-in-an-eternity view of the back of God. Talk about a "brush with Greatness"! Nothing even comes close.

It was quite obvious something unusual happened to Moses on the mountain. Unbeknown to him, when he descended from the mountain, "the skin of his face shone because he had been talking with God" (Ex. 34:29). He glowed! I'm not sure if he glowed in the dark, but all the people were afraid to come near him, so he put a veil over his face. Whenever he went into the Tent of Meeting to meet with God, he'd remove the veil, then put it back on while speaking to the people.

You've seen Christians like this with their humble, loving, Christ-like spirit that gives off a glow. Typically, they are older believers, maybe retired missionaries or pastors and wives. Perhaps they are godly laymen and women who now glow because they have gotten so close to their Lord by spending time in His word and prayer. I've known some young adults who exude this characteristic as well. Maybe they're like Stephen whose "face was like the face of an angel" (Acts 6:15).

When we are with the Lord on a continual basis, it causes us to be obedient and develops a holiness that is unmatched in any other way. You can't produce this on your own, as the seven sons of Sceva found out, or purchase it as Simon tried to do. This is the unconscious influence of God's glory shining through you.

Pritchard also called this the ripple effect. When you throw a rock into a lake, the ripples emanate from the spot where the rock entered the water. The more time you spend with God, the closer you are to Him, where the rock goes in the water, the greater the ripple effect will be seen in your life.

Do you want to get off the roller coaster? Do you want to be used by God so that you can win a lost friend or relative to Christ? Get to know God. Grow in Him. Spend time reading, studying, memorizing and meditating upon God's Word. Anything short of that will leave you teetering on the edge of spiritual bankruptcy.

Clean Jars

Why is obedience so important for witnessing?

The old-time preacher would declare God doesn't want to use dirty jars. He would be partially quoting from 2 Timothy 2, where the Apostle Paul tells Timothy there are various vessels in a house – "some of gold and silver but also of wood and clay, some for honorable use, some for dishonorable" (vs. 20). The exhortation for Timothy, and us, is to allow God to clean us so that we each "will be a vessel for honorable use, set apart as holy, useful to the master of the house, ready for every good work" (vs. 21).

It makes sense. God would prefer to use clean, acceptable vessels as soul-winners. Wouldn't you, if you were in His shoes? If you had the choice of who would represent you to a lost and dying world, wouldn't you choose someone who was living a life pleasing to you, as opposed to a person living in total disobedience? The answer is quite obvious. God desires to use the vessels of honorable use.

If I can be a bit transparent—when I'm not walking with Christ as I should, when I'm disobeying His commands, not having fellowship with Him, struggling in my prayer life, in conflict with my wife and family, and captivated by sins which cling so closely (Heb. 12:1)—witnessing is the furthest thing from my mind. I am not "ready in season or out of season" (2 Tm. 4:2). I'm hoping to avoid the subject of salvation with unbelievers. But when my walk with Christ is humming, I'm ready to go.

So how about you? Are you a vessel God delights in using? Or are you one that is set on the "dishonorable" shelf? Are you spending time with God so that your life is glowing? May I challenge you to do a self-evaluation of your relationship with Christ, and then make the changes to be that honorable vessel.

Soul-winning is going right for the jugular of the enemy. We may not be encountering a demon or a legion of demons, but snatching someone from the grip of their father the devil is a spiritual battle indeed. Therefore, we need to go in the power of God. It begins with obedience to Him. Then ...

For Further Thought:

1. Are you a vessel God delights in using? Or are you one set on the "dishonorable" shelf? Do a self-evaluation of where you stand with Christ, and then make the changes necessary to be that honorable vessel.
2. Would your friends tell you there is or is not a difference between the way you live and the way they live?
3. When you are asked to share about your relationship with God, is it past tense or as current as today?
4. If you bowed the knee to Christ and did exactly what you knew He desired, now, with the right heart attitude, what would that action be?

4

Tapping Into The Source
For Power, Press Prayer
Acts 3:1-10; 4:23-31

The flash mob started in Solomon's Portico at the temple. A noisy religious fanatic was praising God and claiming he had just been healed. As the crowd gathered, two men began to preach. They gave credit to Jesus for the miracle and then charged the people with His death. "You killed the Author of life, whom God raised from the dead" (Acts 3:15). "Repent, therefore, and turn again, that your sins may be blotted out" (vs. 19).

This did not sit well with the religious leaders who immediately and on the spot arrested them, putting them in custody for interrogation the next day.

The entire ordeal began when Peter and John innocently entered the Temple "at the hour of prayer, the ninth hour" (Acts 3:1). They happened upon a lame beggar at the gate.

Beggars Among Us

Beggars are seen in all parts of the world at all times. Some are down on their luck; others descended to this place via alcohol and drugs; some are stuck in a cycle of governmental dependence and then there are others who are outcasts because of their status in life. This is most notable in India with its outlawed caste system that will not go away. Others have physical or mental disorders that make it challenging for them to work and live in a civil society. Still others think standing at the entrance of a popular place or roadway interchange, holding a sign and seeking handouts, is acceptable work.

I, for one, am conflicted when I encounter people like this. On the one hand, I'd like to help. Perhaps they are angels in disguise. More than likely, they are people in need. Jesus noted we'd always have the poor with us, and therefore we should reach out with compassion to help them. "As you did it to one of the least of these my brothers, you did it to Me" (Mt. 25:40).

On the other hand, I fear whatever monies I give them will be used for nefarious things like alcohol, tobacco, or drugs. On a few occasions I've actually taken down-and-outers to a local fast food joint. My church also developed a plan to help those in need.

This was started in part because of a learning incident early in my ministry. A guy came to the church parsonage telling a tale of woe and in need of cash. I didn't have much, but, remembering my mom giving food to hobos, and as the new local pastor, I knew I needed to do something. So I opened my already thin wallet and gave him some cash. I wished him Godspeed and off he went. A week or so later, another guy showed up at the door. That seemed odd. We had lived at the place for several months and no one had stopped. Now two in such a short time. When I went out on the porch to speak with the gentleman, I saw some rustling in the overgrown bushes. Lo and behold, there was the guy from before. He had brought his buddy to get a free handout. No money was exchanged this time, and I doubt I gave him a proper departing blessing.

Peter and John had no money to give to the lame beggar they met. "Silver and gold have I none; but what I do have I give to you" Peter said (Acts 3:6, KJV). Then he told the man, "In the name of Jesus Christ of Nazareth, rise up and walk!"

That must have been a scary thing for the lame man. He had never walked before. In fact, he couldn't even get up on his own. Peter had to take him by the right hand and raise him up. And that's when the miracle happened – "immediately his feet and ankles were made strong (vs. 7).

This was no magical trick or slight of hand. The beggar was truly lame, even carried by friends to this gate to beg every day. Everyone recognized him. But now, so strong were his feet and ankles in the healing, he leaped and walked and walked and leaped right into the temple with Peter and John (vs. 7-8). His loud praise to God is what drew the crowd.

Why Miracles?

Miracles in the New Testament are fantastic to say the least. Jesus performed so many the Bible could not contain them all (Jn. 20:30). His miracles had several purposes. They proved Jesus was who He claimed to be—God. They proved that as Creator, He had control over all His creation. They also fulfilled prophecy. Theologian R. C. Sproul noted that the aim of miracles is not to prove the existence of God, but rather, to "demonstrate and authenticate a messenger of God."[1]

May I add another non-biblical, but very obvious purpose? Miracles drew a crowd. People had to see what was going on. A blind man was able to walk around without handlers or bumping into things. He could really see! A cripple whose legs might have been deformed from birth with muscle atrophy or nonexistent tissue was able to stand, walk, run, leap, jump, dance, and kick some stones. People who could not hear or speak were now hearing clearly, singing and praising God at the top of their lungs. A person who was dead for several days, to the point of potentially having a strong odor (think decomposing road-kill), came out of the grave. Jesus told the onlookers to "unbind him, and let him go" (Jn. 11:44). If you don't think that grabs the attention of the masses, then you and I are not on the same planet.

If you wish to draw a crowd, forget juggling a few chainsaws—perform some genuine miracles. That may sound farfetched, but it is one reason God gave supernatural powers to the leaders of the first church[2]. They were starting a church from nothing, from the ground floor. Only 120, including the eleven disciples, Mary and Jesus' brothers, were gathered in the Upper

Room to wait and see what would happen. That was it. The multitudes that came to Jesus for healing and to hear Him teach, had gone home—some in belief, others in unbelief (John 6:67). God knew the disciples would need something to draw the attention of the people and substantiate their ministry. The signs and wonders confirmed the truth they were preaching and helped people believe Jesus truly was the Son of God (Mk. 16:20).

Do these miracles continue today? Sometimes I wish they did. I can envision me standing in Times Square with a coffin containing the remains of Elvis (the real one). As I open the lid and command him to rise, he sings, "You ain't nothing but a hound dog." Do you think I'd have a crowd around me? You betcha! I'd be on the Times Square Sony Jumbotron, and in no time, the video would go viral. But that doesn't appear to be the norm in the way God has chosen to work these days. I'm not saying He can't or won't. I've got stories from India which say He does. I'm saying it's rather rare. So leave Elvis in his final resting place in Memphis and don't count on miracles to affirm your message of the Gospel of Jesus Christ.

Oh, there is a miracle that takes place many times every day. Whenever a person comes to a saving knowledge of Jesus Christ, that person who was once spiritually blind, lame, deaf and dead, is now alive, given new birth. There is no greater miracle than that miracle. When you share the Good News of Jesus Christ and your friend receives that gift, you will see a miracle right before your eyes. And you might have a noisy, praising-God-type-of-fanatic on your hands. What a day that will be!

Even for Peter and John in the temple, the greatest miracle they saw was the miracle of salvation. As a result of the healing miracle and Peter's preaching, the number of male believers grew to 5,000 (Acts 4:4). Wow![3]

Bold Witness

The day after this miracle, Peter and John went before a council of the religious leaders, including Ananias and Caiaphas. These "whitewashed walls" (Acts 23:3) were the same two high priests who stood in judgment during the kangaroo courts that sentenced Jesus to death. The disciples were quizzed about the source of the miracle. Boldly, Peter gave all the credit to Jesus Christ. "This Jesus is the stone that was rejected by YOU [emphasis added by me and probably by Peter] … and there is salvation in no one else, for there is no other name under heaven given among men by which we must be saved" (vss. 11–12).

The leaders were astonished that these "uneducated, common men" (vs. 13) had such boldness. They concluded it could only be because they had been with Jesus. The disciples must have learned from Him, they thought. The leaders were befuddled, not knowing what to do with them. Clearly, a miracle had been performed. It was evident to all the inhabitants of Jerusalem, and even the leaders could not deny it (vs. 16).

Maybe this was the beginning of the trend mentioned a few chapters later in Acts: "A great many of the priests became obedient to the faith" (Acts 6:7). The healing of a lame beggar was enough proof that something miraculous was going on. Commoners like Peter and John could not do this on their own. They had been with Jesus, yes! But something else was happening.

At this point, the council slapped them on the wrist, telling them to cease and desist. That warning had a great impact on the disciples. With their tails between their legs, they slouched back to their side of the religious divide, vowing to be silent and no longer speak in Jesus' name.

Are you kidding? This emboldened them even more!

So, from where did that power come? What transformed these common men making them outspoken for God? You have to read the middle of Acts 4 to discover this. After Peter and John were released, they went back to their friends to give a report. Then with one voice they lifted up praise to God and prayed and prayed and prayed and prayed and prayed. "The place in which they were gathered together was shaken, and they were all filled with the Holy Spirit and continued to speak the word of God with

boldness! (vs. 31, emphasis added).

Receiving Power

The power source is God. We should never forget this fact. The power lines needed to tap into this power source, however, are twofold. First was "the Helper" whom Jesus had promised. "And I will ask the Father, and He will give you another Helper, to be with you forever, even the Spirit of truth, whom the world cannot receive, because it neither sees Him nor knows Him. You know Him, for He dwells with you and will be in you" (Jn. 14:16-17). The Holy Spirit came upon the new believers in a big way when they were in the Upper Room and at other times as well. And, thank God, He has never left us! "I will never leave you or forsake you" (Heb. 13:5). That part of the power source is permanently in place, but it requires obedience, a yielded heart and dependence for it to be effective. Dependence upon the Holy Spirit and His power leads us to the second power line—prayer.

The disciples became men of prayer. Before Jesus left them and ascended into heaven, prayer didn't appear to play a huge role in their lives. Oh, they often observed Jesus leaving for a solitary place early in the morning to pray. They saw and heard Him pray. In fact, they were so impressed with His prayers and, perhaps, ashamed of their lack of prayer, that they asked Him to teach them to pray (Lk. 11:1).

Nowhere do we read of them praying. There is one occasion in which Jesus told them to pray. On the night of His arrest when He was so absorbed and grieved by the cup He was going to bear—with the trials and beatings and crucifixion ahead, knowing He would carry the weight of the sin of the world, knowing He would be forsaken by His Father—He desired prayer support from His friends. How did they do? Christ had to wake them up, twice, because they couldn't stay awake to pray for one hour. "Could you not watch one hour? Watch and pray that you may not enter into temptation. The spirit indeed is willing, but the flesh is weak" (Mark 14:37-38).

Tapping Into the Source

I'm not very judgmental on this point because my flesh has often been weak as I've fallen asleep or my mind has wandered during prayer meetings. I remember one specific time during the first week of orientation at Camp Ha-La-Wa-Sa in south Jersey, when I was trying to demonstrate that this preacher's kid was leadership material. During devotions one night, while we were in bed and each taking our turn to pray, I wandered off into never-never land and fell fast asleep. I was aroused by a chorus of guys making fun of me. I hate to admit it, but I've dozed off a time or two during a prayer in a church service. Fortunately, I was not the one praying. Doubly fortunate, Vonnie, my wife, always bumps me before I start to snore!

Prayer was not on the agenda of the disciples when Jesus was on earth. But when He left, they knew prayer was their power source connection. It became the very first thing they did and continued to do. If Jesus, the Son of God, needed to pray, how much more did they need to pray? So they gathered in the Upper Room as one, "devoting themselves to prayer, together with the women and Mary the mother of Jesus, and His brothers" (Acts 1:14).

The power of God in their witnessing, in defending the faith, and in standing up against the antagonistic religious leaders was not only evidence of obedience, it was also a direct result of prayer.

We cannot overstate the significance of prayer in any part of life, but especially in relation to sharing our faith.

The Battle for Souls

The new birth is a dramatic miracle, but not only because of the new condition—the old becoming new. We need to remember that a battle has been raging for that soul. The Evil One does not want to lose a grip on one of his children. He will use whatever is available in his arsenal at the time—doubts, fears, interruptions, distractions, and so forth—to hold fast to what he believes to be his. This is spiritual warfare. We are going up against the archenemy of God to snatch someone from his clutches. Can we do this on our own? Are you kidding? Remember Ralph, Mike, Richard, Henry, George, Forrest and Arnold—the seven sons of Sceva (from chapter three)? All they encountered was one demon in one man. Who knows what we are going up against when we begin to share our faith?

"We do not wrestle against flesh and blood," the apostle Paul noted, "but against the rulers, against the authorities, against the cosmic powers over this present darkness, against the spiritual forces of evil in the heavenly places" (Eph. 6:12). Pastor Troy Calvert wrote – "only a foolish soldier would enter the battlefield without proper preparation or weapons or armor; so, too, it is foolish for any Christian to think it is possible to wage an effective battle for men's souls without first preparing, without first pleading for God's power."[4]

There's another reason why prayer is so important in regard to sharing one's faith. No matter which position you find yourself on the theological continuum concerning salvation,[5] this truth is irrefutable: God is the One doing the saving. We can argue all we want on the free will of man, but know this, salvation is of God (Ps. 68:20; Eph. 1:4-6,11; 2:8-9; Rom. 8:29-30). He calls. He saves. He redeems. He justifies. He gives new life. We don't do any of this. We are merely the instruments God uses to present the truth. God does the saving. That being the case, He must be involved in an intimate way. The way He has chosen for us to communicate with Him, in all areas and especially in sharing our faith, is through prayer.

When we pray for the soul of our loved one, as J. I. Packer noted, we do so under the assumption that God has the power to bring that person to faith. "The irony of the situation is that when we ask how the two sides pray, it becomes apparent that those who profess to deny God's sovereignty really believe in it as strongly as those who affirm it."[6]

Every believer must believe in the importance of prayer for the salvation of their friends and family members.

Prayer Needs

How should we pray in regard to evangelism? First, we should pray for ourselves. We need God's guidance to lead us to the right person at the right time with the right words. God holds the date book for divine appointments. We must pray that we'll be ready and willing. We must pray that God will give us the courage and the words to say. Fear plays a huge role in the reason we do not witness. However, "God has not given us a spirit of fear, but of power and of love and of a sound mind" (2 Tim. 1:7, KJV). We need to pray that He will break through our timidity and give us the boldness to present the Gospel.

D. L. Moody was not only a man of prayer, and arguably the most effective preacher of the second half of the 19th century, he was also a personal soul-winner. He vowed before God, according to his associate R. A. Torrey, "that he would never let twenty-four hours pass over his head without speaking to at least one person about his soul."[7] This vow became a challenge for him at times because he led a busy life. On more than one occasion, Torrey noted, Moody would remember his vow when he was in bed, get out of bed, get dressed and go into the streets to share the Gospel. Often there was a lonely soul outside on the street that night who needed to hear the Good News. Moody was prayed-up and ready "in season and out of season" (2 Tim. 4:2) to share the message of Jesus Christ.

Second, we need to pray for the lost. Pray that God will open the hearts of our Nathanael (loved ones, relatives, neighbors, coworkers), so they will be receptive to the message of salvation. And not, "Lord, save all my friends." Get specific. Name them.

When I was growing up, I had a bedtime prayer I always prayed. I would make various requests – kid requests, but I always concluded with, "Help Uncle Eddie and Aunt Janet to get saved, and help me not to get sick and throw up." That later part of the prayer worked for many, many years. The former continues to be a prayer of mine especially with uncle Eddie. We must pray for others.

So how's your prayer life in regard to unsaved loved ones? How many people did you pray for today in respect to their soul? How often do you pray for your lost friends?

There is one more way I'd like to mention in which prayer can be utilized in sharing our faith—that is to actually pray with a nonbeliever. Our tendency is to hide from our unsaved friends this unique, one-to-one, personal relationship we have with God. When we are eating together, instead of pausing to pray before the meal, as is the Christian custom, we thank God in our heart without closing our eyes or skipping a beat. We'd hate to embarrass ourselves or them. Basically, we are denying who we are when we do this.

During college breaks, I worked for a Christian-owned company that had many unbelievers. We were furniture movers. I had the boldness, as a young budding preacher boy, to bow my head before eating lunch. Inevitably one of the guys would say, "What . . . Dan . . . do you have a headache?" Interestingly, it was always after I prayed. They didn't interrupt the prayer. But how much better it would have been if I had told them that I like to show gratefulness to God for the provision of the meal and if I had asked their permission to pray out loud? That would have been true boldness.

Subsequently when I have done this, I've never had anyone turn me down. Typically, I will include that person in the prayer in a small, simple way: "God, encourage us and meet Arnold's needs this day." If you start this practice now, then later when your friends are going through a crisis or in a time of need, you may be the first person they call, asking you to pray for them. And this may lead to a witnessing experience.

I went to a hospital to visit one of the movers I knew during that time period. He was a crusty old gentleman who was dying of lung cancer (he was a prolific smoker). As he lay in his hospital bed, the only temporary, physical relief he gained was the chipped ice from the Styrofoam cup on the tray table. Oh, there was another relief, a greater relief, the greatest relief, when old Pappy Kline, as we called him, silently received Jesus Christ in prayer while I was there. Did my prayers during lunch have anything to do with his willingness to listen to the Gospel in his last days? I don't know, but I'm looking forward to seeing him in Glory.

In his book *Evangelism and Missions: Strategies for Outreach for the Twenty-first Century*, Dallas Theological Seminary professor, Ronald Blue, tells how a visit to one of the world's largest churches in Korea revealed one way prayer is used in evangelism. Each person who becomes a member of that church makes various commitments. One commitment is the promise that any time a friend, neighbor or relative has a problem, the church member must visit and they will take a gift, usually fruit or flowers, and ask, "We heard about the problem, can we pray?" The member prays right then with them and then leaves. Two or three days later, the member revisits, always with a gift and the request to pray.[8]

The deacon who spoke to Dr. Blue noted that their church has not only seen a lot of answers to prayer, but usually people will ask their Christian friend if they can go to church with them. Church growth via prayer.

Peter and John, Stephen, Philip, the other apostles and many more in that first church saw great power in their lives because of prayer. The apostle Paul believed in prayer as well. Despite the fact that he was a champion of the faith, saw hundreds come to know Christ, started churches everywhere and willingly endured persecution and imprisonment, he realized where the real power source lay. If he were to have any effectiveness, it would only be the result of prayer. As he was winding down his letter to the church at Colossae, he asked the believers to "continue steadfastly in prayer, being watchful in it with thanksgiving. At the same time, pray also for us, that God may open to us a door for the word, to declare the mystery of Christ, on account of which I am in prison—that I may make it clear, which is how I ought to speak" (Col. 4:2-4).

We cannot expect God to work in and through us to lead our Nathanaels to Christ unless we are willing to spend time in prayer

- praying for their souls.

You want fearless power to be able to witness to your friends? Press prayer!

> Power in prayer, Lord, power in prayer,
>> Here 'mid earth's sin and sorrow and care;
> Men lost and dying, souls in despair;
>> O give me power, power in prayer![9]

For Further Thought:

1. Will you simply pray, "Lord, I would really like to share You with _____ (my Nathanael). Please give to me the opportunity?"
2. Will you simply pray, "Lord, open _____ heart to respond" (Acts 16:14).
3. Could you simply pray for the same uncle _____ and aunt _____ family member _____ daily?
4. Will you fervently pray, "Lord, let me speak Your Word with all confidence" (Acts 4:19)?
5. Focus on detailed prayer for your Nate like a laser guided missile.

5

A Duet Turns Delightful
Talk the Walk; Walk the Talk
Acts 16:16-34

S inging while in the shower to a tune in my head—ear-
piercing. Singing my part with a choir or quartet, with piano
accompaniment to keep me on tune—nice. Singing praise and
worship with a praise band and songs I know—fantastic!
Singing after having been severely beaten and with feet in stocks
in a stinking Roman prison—priceless. But I'd rather not go
there.

The story of Paul and Silas singing the night away while
locked up in prison (Acts 16:25) never grows old. It seems odd
they would be doing this, given their circumstances, but it's not
as strange as it might appear. More about that later. First, why
were they there?

On Paul's second missionary journey, he took with him a
man by the name of Silas. Silas (or Silvanus, his given name) is
mentioned several times in the book of Acts, three times in the
introduction of Paul's letters to different churches, and once at the
conclusion of Peter's general epistle. Apparently, he was a quiet
type, since we don't see him slaying giants, calling high priests
"whitewashed walls," or preaching to thousands—at least we
have no record of this. But he was a prophet and preacher, a good
traveling companion, and would have been a valuable member of
any ministerial team. On this occasion he and Paul were headed
to Asia, but God stopped them. They set their sights on Bithynia,

but again they were blocked. In a vision, Paul saw a man from Macedonia who was calling for help. So they boarded a ship and sailed northwest to Samothrace and the following day to Neapolis (16:11). After this they traveled through the area, starting churches as they went. Eventually, they worked their way down to Athens before heading to Jerusalem, making stops along the way.

Trouble often followed them. But that's to be expected. They were attacking the gates of hell and the Evil One was none too happy about it. While in Philippi, they met a girl, possessed by a demon, who was given to fortune-telling. She leeched onto the team, crying out, "These men are servants of the Most High God, who proclaim to you the way of salvation" (16:17). She, and the demon, were correct. That's exactly what the two missionaries were doing. The apostle James noted that demons do indeed believe in God, but they tremble in fear of Him. They do not have saving faith (James 2:19).

The girl's words annoyed Paul so much he finally turned around and rebuked the demon: "I command you in the name of Jesus Christ to come out of her" (Acts 16:18). As a result, the demon left her and the girl was returned to her right mind. This miracle, however, outraged her handlers, who were making easy money from her uncommon ability. They dragged Paul and Silas before the local magistrates, making outrageous and unsubstantiated charges. It worked. The magistrates had Paul and Silas stripped, beaten and thrown into the graybar hotel (vss. 22–23).

Bearing the Unbearable

They could have wished it was a graybar hotel or like one of our prisons. Roman prisons, during Paul's day, were brutal. So deplorable were the conditions that many prisoners begged to be killed rather than imprisoned. Others took their own life at the earliest opportunity. Often the prisons were built in solid rock underground. Thus they were dark, dingy, damp, cold, infested with rodents and other vermin, as well as creepy crawling things.

A Duet Turns Delightful

There were no amenities. No running water, unless you classify what seeped through the walls as "running water." The stench from animal and human excrement must have been unbearably sickening. Add to this Paul and Silas had been brutally beaten, leaving them with open, untreated wounds which would be ripe for infection. In addition, we learn, their ankles were in painful stocks, meaning they had no movement and had to sit in the same filthy spot for, perhaps, hours.

Discouraged? Downtrodden? Not so our heroes. They were singing the night away.

What enabled them to do this?

I once took a ten-hour train ride with a missionary and another U.S. preacher through the heart of India. We paid extra to be in a "sleeper" car. This was not a Pullman, although the lower berths doubled as two beds and the upper berths could make two more. The advantage of being in this car was that it was not nearly as crowded as the rest—think humans and animals stuffed in train cars and hanging out windows, maybe even some on the roof. There were, however, some unpaid and uninvited guests in our car that forced us to remain awake all night—roaches. "There wasn't one roach," as my good friend, Ron Blue says, "they were all married and had lots of children." When the lights went out, they came out to play. The thought of snoring with a roach climbing in and out of our mouths was enough for us to find something to keep us awake. We didn't think singing was a good idea, lest we keep awake our fellow passengers. So each of us, in 30-minute intervals, told a story—any story (true or not)—just to stay awake. We kept that going until we heard the conductor announce our stop.

Paul and Silas had their own reasons for staying awake. The prisons could hold some dangerous criminals. In addition, Paul and Silas were in stocks, making it hard to lie down. We can understand why they did not sleep. But what's with the singing? How could they do that?

Seizing Every Opportunity

John McRay, professor of New Testament and Archaeology at Wheaton College, estimates up to 25 percent of Paul's missionary service may have been spent in prison.[1] He was incarcerated for a short time during our story. He spent two years in jail while in Caesarea and at least another two in Rome, possibly more. Paul states that he experienced "far more imprisonments" than others (2 Cor. 11:23). He possibly spent more time in prison that is not recorded.

Paul didn't perceive prison as something negative. He must have struggled with doubt and fears and wondered why he was holed-up this way. He could be doing so much more on the outside, but he unequivocally states, "I have learned in whatever situation I am to be content" (Phil. 4:11). And contentment was not all he was doing. While imprisoned in Rome, he wrote letters to the churches at Philippi, Colossae, and Ephesus, as well as to Philemon and Timothy. He may have written other letters that have not survived to today. In addition, he was busy sharing his faith with the imperial guards.

Pastor David H. Roper notes these guards were the elite soldiers of their day. They were often young men chosen for their prowess and intellect. These were the leaders of tomorrow who would become commanders in the military and leaders in politics. It so happened (I love the way God works these "so happened" events) these men would be chained to the apostle Paul in four-hour shifts. They would hear the letters to the churches as Paul dictated to his assistant.[2] Not only would the guards hear what was written, but knowing Paul, there is no doubt that he focused his attention on each of them. Paul wrote that the gospel "became known throughout the whole imperial guard" (Phil. 1:13).

Roper notes, "If you were going to evangelize the Roman Empire, you could not pick a more strategic group with which to begin." For four hours Paul had these soldiers captive to hear the Good News of Jesus Christ. "So you begin to wonder," Roper asks slyly, "who was really the prisoner?" He adds that someone once pointed out "Caesar unwittingly became the Chairman for Evangelism of the Roman Empire."[3]

God's ways are not our ways, and our ways are not His ways! Who would have thought Paul's imprisonment would have been so productive for the advancement of the Kingdom of God?

Earthquake!

So Paul and Silas were singing away in this dungeon in Philippi when a strong earthquake rocks the area, flinging the doors off their hinges and loosening the spikes that anchored the chains to the wall. They are free to flee if they chose. Since this took place after Peter had miraculously escaped from prison twice (Acts 5, 12), our heroes may have thought God was at it again, just doing it a bit differently. They could have left. But they did not. They stayed. So did the rest of the prisoners. The jailer, seeing what had become of his jail, and thinking the prisoners had escaped, was about to kill himself. Roman law dictated it was the guard's life for any prisoner that broke free under his care. He may have thought suicide was better than execution, but he was stopped by the reassuring voice of Paul, who informed him all the prisoners remained in the prison and were sitting around a camp fire singing Kumbaya. (OK, that was a bit of writer's embellishment, but all the prisoners were present and accounted for.)

This so impressed the jailer, and realizing all the prisoners stayed because of Paul, that he fell to his knees and asked, "Sirs, what must I do to be saved?" (vs. 30). That night, he and his family placed their faith in Jesus Christ and were baptized.

Talking about the Gospel was Paul's life. He was so committed to Jesus and had such a great love for people that anywhere and everywhere he went, he was ready and willing to share the Good News. I cannot imagine that anyone who crossed his path got away without some sort of witness about Jesus. That's who Paul was.

Remember he had to start from the ground floor with everyone. His procedure was to go to the Jews first, because they at least had a basic understanding of the Messiah. If they rejected him and the Gospel, which was often the case, then it was out to the highways and byways—presenting Jesus Christ to whomever the Lord brought his way. Few, if any, had much of a Biblical background. Most were pagans. So he had to begin at the beginning.

The Challenge Today

In some ways, we face the same challenge—having to begin at the beginning. Most Americans have an opinion about Christianity and the church, but they do not know what we believe. They don't know that their sin and rejection of Christ will keep them out of Heaven. They've heard the name of God and Jesus used in curses and profanity. Hell and the devil aren't real to them. These make for good jokes, movies and scary Halloween costumes. As far as they've heard, Heaven is a bright light people see on operating tables when they have "died" and come back to life. It's peaceful there. They assume all people go to that peaceful place when they die.

Others have had such negative experiences with the church and church people they are not interested in learning anything about Heaven or Hell, death and sin. They've seen church advertisements for "all you can eat pancake breakfasts," "rummage sales" and "bingo." People who attend church on Sunday morning, they theorize, must have extra social needs that are not being satisfied at home, at the job or the local pub.

Others want nothing to do with the church because of the church's position on various issues. A lot of churches, they believe, denounce pleasures everyone else enjoys. Or the churches and Christians pick on the civil rights of people. Not the black-on-white civil rights, necessarily, but the newly defined concept in regard to sexual preferences. The church is homophobic, they would accuse. And, of course, the church is in the womb, interfering with a woman's right to choose. Thus, "you can keep your church and leave your Christianity at home!" they would protest.

Let's face it: we have an uphill fight. We not only have to start at the bottom, but somehow we need to eliminate preconceived notions.

How do we deal with people like this? How do we present the Gospel to those who have negative views, or no view at all, on Christianity and the church?

My wife, Vonnie, and I were talking about this very issue in regard to a woman she knows. When Vonnie first met her and would say something vaguely Christian, she had the deer in the headlights look—a blank stare. She didn't get it, or didn't get Vonnie.

What should she do?

We concluded that this woman needs to be desensitized to Christianity.

Spiritual Desensitizing

You know what it means to desensitize someone? Think how disturbed we are about movies, TV shows and video games that promote sex and violence. Just focusing on violence, researchers say the average child, before he or she is 18, will have seen 200,000 violent acts and 16,000 murders—and that's just on television. This exposure to violence desensitizes people, especially the young and vulnerable. If they see violence in real life, they may not be as concerned because of all the virtual violence they've already experienced.

The same principle holds true for something positive, namely the Gospel. Since nonbelievers have either been fed a steady diet of misinformation concerning the Gospel or know nothing about it, we need to desensitize them to Christianity.

How do we do that? It's simply stated but perhaps harder to implement. Yet, it can be done. We just need to live the life of a true follow of Jesus Christ.

Let me make several suggestions.

Kindness Goes a Long Way

First, we can begin to desensitize people to Christianity by being kind. Paul wrote, "Be kind one to another, tenderhearted, forgiving one another, as God in Christ forgave you" (Eph. 4:32). Being kind should not be limited to just other believers. It should be the pattern of our life.

Jesus was kind. I cannot think of one Biblical example in which He was not. He was firm with the religious leaders and their misinterpretations of God's law which subjugated the Jews with unattainable righteousness. But, He still treated them with respect as He denounced what they were doing. His actions in the Temple—turning over the tables, scattering the money changers and animal hustlers—was righteous indignation, anger. This doesn't really fit on the kind-unkind meter. He treated everyone with value. He came to seek and save the lost. And to do this He needed to be kind.

In the Sermon on the Mount He changed the rules: "You have heard that it was said, 'An eye for an eye and a tooth for a tooth.' But I say to you, . . . if anyone slaps you on the right cheek, turn to him the other also. And if anyone would sue you and take your tunic, let him have your cloak as well. And if anyone forces you to go one mile, go with him two miles" (Matt. 5:38-41). He's talking about being different, showing true Christianity.

We live in a society that has forgotten how to be kind. We've lost the concept of civility. It's a dog-eat-dog, every-man-for-himself type of world. Because of that, living like Christ by being kind may just set us apart from everyone else. It may make us stand out. In fact, you may throw people a curve ball by being kind to them. They might wonder what's up your sleeve, what's in it for you, what do you want from them? We don't want anything from them. We just want to share the greatest story ever told about the greatest Person who ever lived and the greatest news one could ever hear. No selfish motive here—just a lifeline to a person who is spiritually dying. Showing kindness to others could help in breaking down some of the barriers that have been built against Christianity.

Be a Friend

A second way to desensitize people to Christianity is to befriend them. Jesus spent the better part of three years befriending and then teaching His disciples. The boldness of the disciples, as noted in the last chapter, was attributed by the religious leaders to the fact they had been with Jesus. Jesus had rubbed off on these friends of His.

Friend-to-friend evangelism is the most effective way of witnessing. We need the hit-and-run witnessers as well (to be discussed later in the chapter "Tools for Sharing Your Faith"). But that one-to-one relationship with unbelievers is how the majority are brought into the Kingdom—think Paul and those prison guards and the jailer.

I suppose we could ask the question—how can you witness to friends who are unbelievers if you have no unbelieving friends? We might need to be intentional in making friends with those who do not yet know the Lord.

They'll Know We are Christians by ...

Thirdly, we can warm people up to hear the Gospel of Jesus Christ by loving them.

Jesus told the disciples, "A new commandment I give to you, that you love one another: just as I have loved you, you also are to love one another. By this all people will know that you are My disciples, if you have love for one another" (John 13:34-35). Clearly, this command is inward—disciples loving disciples, believers loving on other believers. But we need to view it as more than that. Part of the Jewish law was to "love your neighbor as yourself" (Lev. 19:18). In the parable of the Good Samaritan Jesus identified even the people Jews hated the most, the Samaritans, as neighbors (Luke 10:36-37). He also instructed us to love our enemies (Matt. 5:44). Therefore, love is a mandated distinguishing mark of Christians. It is to set us apart.

British Methodist theologian and Bible scholar, Adam Clarke, wrote, "No system of morality ever prescribed any thing so pure . . . as this. Our blessed Lord has outdone all the moral systems in the universe in [these] words – 'love one another' (John 13:34)."[4]

The early church took this seriously. What made them stand out among all the pagans and religions was their love, often self-sacrificing—not only for each other, but also for outsiders. This love was clearly manifested during the pandemic of the third century. It started around 250 AD and, according to one source, at the height of the outbreak, claimed 5,000 lives a day in Rome. Many Christian historians believe this epidemic is one reason that catapulted Christianity, spreading it throughout the known world.[5]

How so? Well, while nonbelievers were dumping the bodies of their sick family members into the streets before they died (I repeat, before they died!) so that they would not get the same disease, Christians were not only tending for their own sick, but caring for those who had been discarded, often bringing them into their own homes. This was long before the organized mercy ministries of hospitals, the Salvation Army and Samaritan's Purse. It was way before anyone knew anything about germs and infectious diseases. Christians were actually dying alongside those they helped. And they did so willingly. They were driven to love even the unlovable. The pagan world around them saw this. They knew there was something different about Christians.

The youth song from the '60s rings in my ears: "They'll know we are Christians by our love, by our love, yes they will know we are Christians by our love."

That kind of love and care needs to permeate our Christian relationships and be seen by the outside world. If the woman to whom Vonnie wishes to witness will see genuine, spiritual love for her and for others, it should soften her so that Vonnie can go to the next step—sharing the hope that is within her. This step of love is often called lifestyle evangelism.

A Duet Turns Delightful

Loving someone like this is walking the walk of Jesus. God so loved us He sent His Son to die on the cross for our sins. Jesus' love was evident to everyone with whom He came in contact. Walking the walk is loving people.

Talking the Talk

A final suggestion for desensitizing a nonbelieiver to Christianity is tell them about the Good News.

When Vonnie's friend gave her the deer-in-the-headlights look whenever she talked about Christian things, the question was—should she stop talking that way? Should she not say she will pray for this person and her family when a need is presented? Should she not hum Christian songs that are in her head? Should she try to be more worldly in her relationship with this person? The answer is an emphatic NO! We don't want to push Christianity on a person. We don't want to be obnoxious— pricking people by constantly preaching at them. If that's your style, STOP! It doesn't work. It turns people away and means someone else down the line will have to desensitize them from your pseudo-Christian testimony. On the other hand, we must not put our light under a basket either. It needs to shine, brightly!

In His Sermon on the Mount, Jesus spoke about being a light. "You are the light of the world" (Mt. 5:14).[6] It wasn't "Some of you will be the light of the world," or "I've chosen some pastors and missionaries to be that light." No, he emphatically states, "**YOU** are the light of the world"! Each one of us, who names the name of Jesus, is light. Unfortunately, the light of many is the size of a flickering, miniature birthday candle that can barely be seen across a darkened room. We need to be a spotlight shining the way. We do this by acting, living and talking like a Christian. Jesus said, "In the same way," as a city on a hill can be seen by everyone, and a lamp is put on a stand, "let your light shine before others, so that they may see your good works and give glory to your Father who is in Heaven" (Mt. 5:15-16).

A Duet Turns Delightful

Before we can talk about someone's sin and their eternal destiny and before we can share the Good News of Jesus Christ, we may need to desensitize them to Christianity. Might being kind, befriending unbelievers, and showing love, allow us to talk the talk?

Midnight Duet

So, at midnight, Paul and Silas were praying and singing hymns in the jail. Did you ever wonder how the singing got started? There was no striking up the praise band. No one said, "Now turn to page 57 in your hymn books." No piano or keyboard to set the tune. How might it have started? Maybe they entered the prison singing to rejoice "that they were counted worthy to suffer dishonor for the name" (Acts 5:41).

Or perhaps it was something like this. Paul, sitting close to Silas and in terrible pain, gives a longer than usual moan. Silas, perhaps with an ear for music, picks up on the tone and with his own moaning hums a few notes of a familiar hymn. They both begin to chuckle and then laugh, but it hurts too much to laugh. So they latch onto that hum and slowly, in between moans, keep humming the tune they knew so well. And then Paul starts adding the words, and Silas joins him. Soon the music swells deep inside of them as they think of their precious Lord and all He means to them. Louder and louder and louder the songs from deep in their souls comes out as they harmonize. From one hymn to another they praise the Lord. Unashamed. Unabashed. Interspersed with prayers. They no longer feel the pain, as all the energy they can muster goes into singing and praying to God.

This is who Paul and Silas were. This is why the prisoners did not escape when they had the opportunity. And this is why the jailer wanted what Paul and Silas had as he said, "What must I do to be saved?" This was one duet that turned delightful!

Walk the walk. Talk the talk. Live like Jesus.

For Further Thought:

1. If a man came to a home carrying pipe and plumbing supplies, we'd know him as a plumber. If a man with grease on his hands and wrenches was under the hood of a car, we'd know him as a mechanic. What tools do you use to demonstrate God's reality in your life?

2. What are two practical services you could provide to those who may know or should know you as a follower of Jesus Christ?

3. Can a demonstration of love be disputed? Can its motives?

4. What would it look like to you for someone to show that your best interest was at stake with them? Turn it around.

5. If you love your neighbor as yourself, how do you love yourself?

6. Is there power provided by the Spirit for you to fulfill His intentions for others through me?

The Nathanael Project

Everybody has a Nathanael

"The Nathanael Project" is a 2-month-long (9 Sunday) church-evangelism program that includes everyone in your church—from children in Primary and Junior Church, to teens and adults. The program consists of an easy-to-read book on evangelism: *Exhaling the Gospel of Jesus Christ . . . Evangelism as Natural as Breathing the Truth*; a daily & family devotional booklet which also includes the Small Group guide; curriculums for children and teens; lessons for Adult Sunday School and Small Groups; a short video for each Small Group session as well as sermons for the pastor. The goal is for everyone to pray for, and learn how to share Jesus with, their Nathanael (friend, co-worker, class-mate, neighbor, relative), because "Everyone Has a Nathanael" . . . someone who needs to be brought to Jesus (John 1:45).

6

Game On!
What Position Are You Playing?
Acts 17:16-34

The more the merrier might have been the creed of the court of Areopagus. This esteemed body of men in the city of Athens, along with many others, would sit around all day chewing the fat and talking about new things (Acts 17:21). Religion was one of the themes they liked to converse.

The vast majority of people in the world believe there is some sort of god or gods. One doesn't need a Gallup poll or Pew research to learn this. It's obvious by even a cursory look at countries and tribes. The way of worship might be sophisticated, as in an organized religion with priests, temples, icons and idols, or it could be tribal lore, traditions and customs. Often the "gods" are utilized to explain the unexplainable. Where does the rain come from? Without meteorologists or an understanding of the science of the water cycle, people might assume there is a rain god. This can go for all unexplained things—from meteorites that land near a tribe (Acts 19:35), to the sun, to animals that are feared, and even people.

Hinduism boasts of either 33 million or 330 million gods—depending on the translation of one word within the number. But who's counting? Others say the large number represents the infinite forms of god. Thus, one can never really know how many gods exists since the list can be increased at almost any time as more gods are identified and added. My size, rather large, could put me into a "god" category with some Indians. Most have never seen someone so large. Fortunately, they do not throw flowers and rice at me . . . although doughnuts and Rupees would be accepted.

While spending time wandering the streets in Athens, Paul encountered "a forest of gods." In front of homes and walkways stood pillars with the bust of Hermes, the god of roadways, gateways and the marketplace.[1] The writer of Acts, Dr. Luke, wrote that Paul's "spirit was provoked within him as he saw that the city was full of idols" (17:16).

Paul's strategy to witness to these "thinkers" would need to be different than what he used with others. To the Philippian jailor, who was desperate to hear what made Paul different, he must have presented the Gospel in very simple terms. That's all the jailer and his family needed. When speaking to Jews in the synagogue on a Sabbath, Paul would open up the Old Testament to prove that Jesus was the Messiah. We don't know all he said to Lydia down by the river, but it would have been different from what he said to the men of Athens. They were philosophers. He needed something to grab their attention.

The Unknown God

I always enjoy watching talented professionals display their craft. It's poetry in motion. Paul fit that description. But he did not blow the Athenians out of the water with philosophical precepts. Rather, he caught their attention in a simple and unique way.

As Paul walked throughout the city, he saw an altar, maybe more than one, with the inscription, "To the unknown god" (vs. 23). There are various theories as to whom or what this represented. These could have been altars to help identify ancient burial sites, which were disturbed during building projects of later generations. Perhaps people thought this would stave off any repercussions for disturbing the dead. Another theory suggests these altars identified locations of sacrifices to stop a sixth century B.C. plague. It mattered little to Paul. He had his opening line, his icebreaker, to use among these sour and stoic-looking philosophers and religious thinkers.

"Men of Athens," Paul began, "I perceived that in every way you are very religious" (vs. 22). Often it's wise to start out in a non-offensive, positive manner. Much better than saying, "You pagans and children of the devil who will be splitting hell wide open if you don't listen to me . . ." That might be appropriate at times, although I cannot think of any. It certainly will not endear you to the listeners, the very ones you hope to love into the Kingdom, nor does it fit in the "wise as serpents and harmless as doves" category Jesus instructed the disciples to follow (Mt. 10:16).

Paul continued, "I see among your many objects of worship that you have an altar to an unknown god. It is that God whom I represent." He went on to introduce them to the God of the Bible, His Son, Jesus Christ and His resurrection. The results: some were convinced he was crazy and mocked him, especially the Epicurean philosophers, who believed resurrection is physically impossible. Others liked what they heard. "We will hear you again about this, Kemosabe," they said (Acts 17:32). Well, they didn't actually say "Kemosabe," but in my mind I'm seeing some big native Americans with blankets thrown over their shoulders as they sit around a camp fire smoking a peace pipe. I'm sure it did not look like that . . . at least not the pipes.

Finally, there was a group that did more than agree in principle, they joined Paul and believed. This included Dionysius and a woman named Damaris (vs. 34).

Communication Methods

Dr. Elmer Towns is famous for saying, "Methods are many, principles are few; methods may change, but principles never do." This is so true when sharing the Good News of Jesus Christ. The way we talk to children varies from how we speak to teens, and is often vastly different from our approach to adults. Likewise, we don't speak to laborers and college professors in the same way.

Game On!

I recall one of my first witnessing encounters, which took place at night on the beach in Ocean City, NJ. It was break day for us workers from the children's camp (Camp Ha-La-Wa-Sa). After a little swimming, some boardwalk food (pork roll or Philly cheese steaks, fries and saltwater taffy), we handed out tracts and witnessed in the evening. I don't recall if we received any training - probably not. The very first person I encountered was a college student majoring in philosophy. Here was a hotshot, pimply-faced 13-year-old preacher's kid, who thought he had the world by its tail, speaking to someone at least eight years his senior who was delving into the likes of John Locke, Epicurus, Plato and Immanuel Kant. I was still very much into Mighty Mouse, Rocky and Bullwinkle, as well as other Saturday morning cartoons while I ate my cereal in front of the TV. I couldn't carry this guy's intellectual water bucket. It was no contest. He shot me out of the water. I moved on quickly to someone else, anyone else. The fact of the matter is, if I met the same guy today, he might still be able to run cerebral circles around me. I'd need to brush up on apologetics, that's for sure.

Paul's methods matched the way Jesus communicated. When Jesus met with the Pharisee named Nicodemus, He answered his questions and did so on a level that would challenge the thinking of a highly trained religious leader. Conversely, Christ's encounter with the woman at the well featured a discussion of water—living water. When He walked along the shore of Sea of Galilee, He engaged the fishermen by talking about fishing. "Follow Me and I'll make you fishers of men" (Matt. 4:19). Moreover, when He was near shepherds or farmers, it was sheep or crops, respectively. Jesus used what was at hand to begin His teachings. Paul used what he had to launch into a presentation of the Gospel.

Both Paul and Jesus were communicators. Paul certainly had the gift of evangelism. And Christ—well, He is perfect in everything He does, including knowing the needs of people and scratching them right where they itch.

Game On!

Finding Your Approach

When learning of my writing this evangelism book, a good friend and pastoral colleague, John Vandegriff, insisted I read Bill Hybels' and Mark Mittelberg's book *Becoming a Contagious Christian*. I had just completed Hybels' book entitled *Just Walk Across the Room*, so this seemed like a good next step. The two authors identified several different styles or approaches in witnessing. I'd like to summarize these approaches demonstrating my proclivity toward sermonic alliteration. Each begins with the same letter. Sorry about that, but that's what I do.

We'll call the approach Jesus and Paul used **Seizing the Moment**. Hybels called this technique the "intellectual approach." This is the ability to take anything around you or something someone says and turn it into a witnessing opportunity. I'm not talking about sitting beside someone on a plane and saying, with a stern voice and a serious look on your face, "If this plane goes down, I'm going up. How about you?" That might fit under the next approach, but we're looking for something a bit softer, not so dramatic. Paul used the gods on Mars Hill. Christ illustrated with whatever was around Him at the time.

Personally, I enjoy when people ask me how I am doing. My patent answer is, "Better than I deserve." This phrase has been popularized by financial expert and radio talk show host, Dave Ramsey. He uses it with the same purpose in mind. We are better than we deserve because if God gave us what we truly deserved, we'd spend eternity separated from God.

Using this phrase often leads into some interesting conversations. Some people argue with me: "Oh, no, everyone deserves the best!" Then I reply, "Well, that's interesting, but there's a good reason why I am better than I deserve. Would you like to know why?" I have had the opportunity to share Christ using this method more times than I can remember. It has never directly led to a person dropping to his or her knees and accepting the Lord, but it is a part of the process of exposing people to the Gospel, planting the seed. Evangelist Bill Fay says on average people must hear the gospel 7.6 times before they place their trust in Jesus.[2] Elmer Towns noted it as the Law of 3 Hearings and 7 Touches.

I'm also able to invite the person to check out the 800FollowMe.com website, where I give a seven-minute explanation of what this means. Incidentally, on the same website, Dave Ramsey explains why God should let anyone into Heaven.

The second approach is the one you could use on the airplane, but please don't be obnoxious. Saying, as David Platt noted: "You're a damned and dreadful sinner in need of salvation," is not going to cut it with most or any. Platt quipped – "The only thing that person will want to be saved from is you."[3]

We'll call this the **Straightforward Approach**. Ron Blue identifies this as "cold calling," but, as he says, he likes to warm people up first. He uses a formula (FORM) to engage them: Family, Occupation, Religion, Message. (More on this in the chapter - "Tools For Sharing Your Faith")

The example Hybels gives is of the Apostle Peter. Does the phrase: "Bull in a China Shop" mean anything to you? Peter was very direct. That may be why Christ chose him to be the initial leader of the pack. Here was a guy who, to our knowledge, had never done any public speaking. He was a fisherman. He had no organized schooling or training, other than sitting at the feet of Jesus. But what better place to sit? From day one of Christ's departure, he was the lead spokesperson for the entire movement. He did a splendid job. I'm not sure any of the other disciples could have pulled this off.

The "Straightforward" approach is something pastors, because of their position, can do with impunity. It is almost expected of us to be direct and ask the difficult spiritual questions. I can walk into a hospital room and, without being thrown out by relatives, can ask a patient, "Have you made your peace with God?" They would expect nothing less.

For others, this approach may seem daunting. It requires, not only the boldness of a Type-A personality, but extensive knowledge. You'd better know what you're talking about and have answers to any or most questions that come at you. You must be ready to defend the faith. There are few things worse than barging in and appearing to be in total control, only to wimp out like a whipped pup because you have no idea what you are saying or should say next.

When Softer Is Better

The next three approaches are a bit softer. The first would be the **Set Up**—you set people up to hear the Good News. Maybe, like the tax collector, Levi (Luke 5:29), you invite all your friends to your house for dinner and bring in someone with the "straightforward" approach to present the Gospel.

Businessman Arthur DeMoss was famous for doing this very thing. The man who started out as a bookie and ran two profitable Albany, NY, "horse rooms," came to know Christ during a tent revival at the age of 25. Subsequently, he became the founder of one of the world's largest mail order insurance companies, but was "burdened that so little was being done to share Christ effectively within the neglected minority of senior executives and influencers."[4]

DeMoss would invite as many as 500 people to his suburban Philadelphia estate to hear Christian celebrities, sports figures and world renowned preachers share their testimonies and present the Gospel. He had a specific step-by-step formula for running these "Outreach Dinner Parties." After the motivational talk and testimony of what Christ meant to the speaker, the guests were invited to make a decision for Jesus Christ. A card was distributed on which they could indicate their decision and request follow-up. Between 30 and 40 percent would indicate they made a decision that night or would like more information.[5]

This is a great approach, especially if you have money and a large house. One time, as a hired mover, I saw the basement of the DeMoss mansion. We were there to collect from storage some furniture of a DeMoss employee. The basement was as large as, and looked like, a department store. Few of us could host outreach dinners on the DeMoss level, but could this concept work on a smaller scale? Why not? You could invite a few people over to your house for dessert and have your pastor come or invite a Christian business person to share his/her testimony. What a tremendous way to present the Gospel to your friends. The "Set Up" approach can be very effective.

On its heels is the **Summoner** approach. This involves people who are willing to invite their friends to church or a special function to hear about Christ. It is similar to what the Samaritan woman did after she met Jesus. "Come, see a Man who told me all that I ever did. Can this be the Christ?" (Jn. 4:29).

In the later part of the 20th century, Elmer Towns and Larry Gilbertson created an organized packet of material to help churches conduct a Friend Day, followed up by the program "FRANtastic Days." The goal for Friend Day, as identified by the name, was for church folks to invite their friends to a service at their church specifically geared toward presenting the Gospel. The second plan consisted of a month of Sundays, one each for Friends, Relatives, Business Associates and Neighbors. The 800FollowMe Church-Evangelism Program utilizes some of this material with "The Nathanael Project" (see add on page 184). When done correctly, friends come, they hear the Gospel, and many put their faith in Jesus Christ. It all boils down, however, to the Samaritan woman types, the **Summoners**, who actually invite their friends. Christian concerts, conferences or special outreaches would all fit within this genre, providing the Gospel is presented. Years ago we filled the church van taking folks to a Billy Graham crusade. At least one lady from our group walked the aisle that evening.

We'll call the next technique the **Service** approach. Hybels uses Tabitha or Dorcas from Acts 9 as the prototype. She was known to be "full of good works and acts of charity" (vs. 36). Doing good deeds and acts of kindness should be the identifying mark of every Christian, but there are some who use this as an outreach. They are known for their benevolence and care for people.

One of my elders, now with the Lord, demonstrated this in a unique way. Late one evening, I received a call that the business of another elder was on fire, literally burning down. From the hillside on my drive, about five miles away, I could see the glow of the fire. It was a large building and by the looks of it, even from a distance, it would be a total loss. I went to encourage my elder, if I could find him. If the truth be known, I went there more to gawk—to see the fire. This other elder, however, when he heard the news of the fire, packed his pickup with plywood and carpenter tools. He came to help. That's who Jim Rennix was—a helper, one who would show acts of kindness. And he did this not just with believers, but also with those who needed to hear the Gospel. He was a soul-winner through acts of kindness, the "Service" approach.

We do not do good deeds solely out of altruistic motives. We do it because we are commanded to love others and behind that is our desire to demonstrate the love of Christ so that the other person may come to a saving knowledge of Jesus. These acts of kindness, the "Service" approach, only work in bringing people to Christ if you explain the reason for the hope that is within you.

The following quote has been attributed to St. Francis of Assisi: "Preach the Gospel at all times and, when necessary, use words." I like the "at all times" and the connection we can make to the service aspect. The "when necessary" part, however, makes it sound as if we can get away with just living the life and doing good deeds and people will get saved. Well, it so happens, according to FactChecker Glenn T. Stanton, St. Francis may have never made this statement.[6]

The problem with St. Francis' quote is not whether or not he said it, but the implication that our living example is enough. The apostle Paul was clear when he wrote, "How are they to call on Him in whom they have not believed? And how are they to believe in Him of whom they have never heard? And how are they to hear without someone preaching?" (Rom. 10:14). The case of Christ and salvation needs to be made. It needs to be verbalized. Those who use the "Service" approach will need to add to this a way to present the Gospel.

Telling Your Story

The last tactic which every Christian should be able to use is called the **Story** approach. This is exemplified in the life of one of the blind men Jesus healed. The healing happened to take place on the Sabbath, which spiked the ire of the religious leaders. They hauled this formerly blind man into their religious council and demanded an explanation—"what happened to you? At this point he wasn't quite sure. He didn't know who Jesus Christ was and therefore could not speak to that. All he knew was "I was blind, now I see" and that's what he told them (Jn. 9:25). After he was expelled from the council, he ran into Jesus again. This time, there was more interaction and he placed his faith in Christ. My guess is, he went about Jerusalem telling his story to people.

Telling your story is a great way of presenting the Gospel, especially if you were converted as an adult. I have a friend who ran a brothel before coming to Christ. What a story to tell! But your story doesn't need to titillate. If you have one of these types of testimonies, make sure you spend more time on the "after" picture and what Christ did for you, as opposed to the "before" picture. The fact is, once you were spiritually blind and now you can see. Once you were dead in your trespasses and sins and now, since Jesus Christ came into your life, you are alive and have the gift of eternal life.

Many of us were saved as children. I was about 5 years old when I went forward at the end of a Sunday evening service in my dad's church in southwest Philadelphia, PA. The district superintendent of our denomination, was that evening's preacher. He was a very big man with what appeared to be oversized forehead and hands (at least that's the perspective of a little lad). But he didn't scare me—what he preached did. There was no way I wanted to go to Hell. So, at the conclusion of the service, C.E. Kirkwood and my dad, both big men, sat on either side of little old me. I remember my dad saying: "Danny do you understand what this means?" In childlike faith, I did.

I'm glad I trusted Christ at such an early age. But my story doesn't help when witnessing to an adult who is struggling with alcoholism, has financial troubles, or lost his family or job. People like this cannot relate to a five year old's conversion experience.

Evangelism Explosion taught us to share how knowing Jesus has impacted our lives as an adult. My E. E. testimony began something like this: "I'm thankful that I have the gift of eternal life because of the peace that it gives me especially in times of grief. My dad was suddenly killed at the age of 50 and I was devastated, but God . . ."[7] (see testimony, page 89. For more information about telling your story, see page 90)

If you know Jesus Christ as your Savior and Lord, you have a story to tell as well. This should be one of the approaches you use. 800FollowMe.com is setting up a virtual platform for you to do this. Contact us at www.800FollowMe.com. (see page).

It is important, as Hybels points out, that you be yourself. There's no cookie-cutter approach to witnessing. It might be a hybrid of some of these approaches or something completely different that works. Providing it's legal and not immoral or theologically incorrect, go for it. Use it.

Wonder Woman Witness

Back in the '80s when I was young and raring to go, I was trained to be a leader in *Evangelism Explosion* at the First Baptist Church of Fort Lauderdale, Florida. One of the advantages of E.E. – in additions to its two questions and thorough outline (See "Tools for Sharing Your Faith")—is what they call OJT (On the Job Training). We didn't just get book knowledge in a classroom, but a trainer would take two very nervous trainees into the field. I had the jitters. So did my friend and parishioner, Chuck Albert. And the trainer they gave us didn't assuage our fears. One would have thought this big preacher would have been assigned to the leader of the seminar or one of the pastors of the church, certainly an elder or deacon. That didn't happen. The person designated to train us was our polar opposite. Chuck and I were from the northeast, tall and perhaps a bit overweight. (Okay, we were overweight.) The trainer was from Florida, short and lean. We were big, bruising guys with beards; she was a petite, soft-spoken schoolmarm. I think she taught fourth grade.

She didn't have the opportunity to explain the Gospel at the first house. It was a good, quick visit as she thanked the family for coming to church and invited them back. She made a good contact for the church, but that was about it. At the second and only other place we went, I saw this woman turn from mild mannered Olive Oyl to Wonder Woman, and she didn't need a phone booth or to spin in a circle for the change. The man, in his late 50s or early 60s, heard the Gospel presentation and responded positively. Then he told us he had a loaded pistol on his night stand. He had planned on taking his life later that evening, but now he had found a reason to live. Wow! This small, diminutive lady very calmly handled the situation and led that man to a saving knowledge of Jesus Christ.

At the roundup time back at the church, she testified about what all had happened. All were amazed and praised the Lord. If this was some secular sales training course, I'd think it was staged, a setup. But I saw that woman in action. She loved Jesus. She loved her family. She loved her fourth graders. And she loved sharing her faith. She was very effective. She did it her way.

I don't know anything about you. If you are a follower of Jesus Christ, then you are my brother or sister. I do know this—the same Jesus who died on the cross for your sin and mine, died on the cross for your Nathanael's sins as well. And that same Jesus desires for them to become part of His family (2 Pet. 3:9). So figure out what approach you are going to use and get busy!

For Further Thought:

1. Which approach for you will be most natural, comfortable, or best at when sharing Christ?
2. What is your greatest barrier to communicating Christ? Does it differ with the individual or setting?
3. What is the worst that could happen when you witness to someone using one of the methods in this chapter?
4. Do you see a method that would work with your Nate?
5. On a deeper level, how could you learn more about their world?

E. E. Personal Testimony
by Dan Allen (1985)

I am glad that I have eternal life because of the peace that God has given to me.

We all go through troubles and heart-aches. I've had a few. Several years ago I received the dreaded phone call that a loved one has died. It happened to be my dad who was killed in an accident by a person on drugs. Dad was only 50 years old. He was my best friend.

At first I was shocked. Although it took a while to grieve, God gave me a simple verse—"Be still and know that I am God." What a comfort that was. There was a feeling from God that everything was okay. He fulfilled another verse by giving to me "a peace that passes understanding."

I've performed funerals for people who did not know if they were going to heaven when they died. It is such a sorrowful thing. But at my dad's funeral there was an assurance that although he was no longer with us, he was with God and we would see him again.

I'm glad that I have that same assurance, that same peace. May I ask you a question? (2 E. E. questions)

Telling Your Story

The President of Evangelism Explosion International, Dr. John Sorensen, asks the question—"When's the last time you shared your testimony with someone?"* He proceeds to encourage Christians about using their testimony as a witnessing tool.

"The substance of our personal testimony," he writes, "is about God's faithfulness in our life. So, when we prepare our testimony for sharing, we're fashioning a Gospel tool to be a more proficient witness for Him. And yet, many Christians have never created their testimony because they don't realize the impact it can have."

To show the importance of sharing one's testimony he cites, Rev. 12:11—"And they have conquered him by the blood of the Lamb and by the word of their testimony, for they loved not their lives even unto death." He notes: "So, your story matters to God and He says He'll use it to defeat Satan in your life and in the lives of those you share it with. Wow! That's pretty amazing."

Evangelism Explosion provides a free testimony building web-site: WhatsMyStory.org. Why not take advantage of this so that you can tell your Nathanael about "the hope that is in you" (1 Pet. 3:15)?

* http://evangelismexplosion.org/your-personal-testimony/

7

A Dream that Changed the World
A Coordinated Effort
Acts 10

The story of Peter, a Christian Jew, witnessing to Cornelius, a righteous Gentile, is filled with things I love – dreams, food and souls saved.

The disciples who joined Christ came with the baggage of the Jewish religion and all its do's and don'ts. Jesus was a Jew; therefore, He abided by the law of Moses. He kept a strict Jewish diet. He went to the Temple when He was supposed to. I'm guessing He presented sacrifices of thanksgiving—He had no sins that required an atonement sacrifice. He did break a few ceremonial rules, but for righteous and just reasons: He touched lepers, was accused of working on the Sabbath (by healing people), let the adulterous woman live (by law she should have been stoned), forgave the Samaritan woman who had five husbands and was living with someone outside of wedlock (another potential stoning), and let the disciples pick handfuls of grain on the Sabbath. They weren't farming, but as they walked through the fields they picked and ate. He didn't stop them.

Jesus always honored the moral law of God, but He objected to the extra Pharisaical rules that so burdened the Jewish people. God had given them ten laws, otherwise known as the Ten Commandments. Added to this were the laws outlined in the

Pentateuch, called the Mosaic law. But the religious leaders, like many people in power, or in their case—self-righteous, self-appointed arbitrators of understanding and interpreting God's law, caused this to balloon into hundreds of rules.[1] It was impossible for anyone except Jesus to keep the Mosaic law, not to mention the extra rules. It was even impossible to know them all.

Since all of the disciples and initial followers of Jesus were converted Jews, it was only natural for them to keep trying to follow Jewish law. That is why a council was needed to determine if Christian Gentiles should be circumcised in keeping with Jewish law (Acts 15).

Two of the major laws the early followers maintained were dietary restrictions and separation from Gentiles. It was a non-disciple, Philip the deacon, who took the first step to break the latter law by taking the Gospel to the Samaritans (Acts 8:5-8). This was not totally out of the realm of possibility because Christ had already spoken with, and brought to Himself, a Samaritan woman (Jn. 4). But it was still a stretch to reach out to these half-breeds (half Jew and half Gentile). When the apostles realized the Samaritans "had received the Word of God, they sent to them Peter and John, who came down and prayed for them that they might receive the Holy Spirit" (Acts 8:14-15).

The Coming of the Spirit

This fact about receiving the Holy Spirit warrants a special note. Several times in the book of Acts the Holy Spirit was not imparted to new believers until the Apostles laid hands on them. What gives? Are you saved first and then later receive the Holy Spirit? After you share your faith with someone and that person trusts in Christ, does he or she have to wait for a special visitation from the Holy Spirit, or the laying on hands from apostles or prophets? No and no!

The book of Acts is a transitional piece from Judaism to the church. Many Christians continued observing Jewish laws and practices until they made a complete break from Judaism. For instance, the apostle Paul made a vow, possibly a Nazarite vow (Acts 18:18-21), which was completed at the temple. The Temple was still held in high honor. Often churches met in Synagogues. And dietary laws continued to be observed.

The imparting of the Holy Spirit was another part of that transition. On four separate occasions in the book of Acts, the Holy Spirit came in a demonstrative, experiential way. Jesus had promised, "You will receive power when the Holy Spirit has come upon you" (Acts 1:8). And, wow, did they! The disciples marched out of the Upper Room and into the throngs of people, presenting the Good News of Jesus Christ while miraculously speaking the languages of the visitors who had come to Jerusalem to worship God. Thousands were added to the church. What a successful impromptu crusade—an evangelistic flash mob!

The second reception of the Spirit involved the Samaritans. As previously mentioned, Jews and Samaritans did not get along. For 500 years they had worshiped at different locations—the Jews in Jerusalem and the Samaritans at Mount Gerizim. Jewish Christians at first may have thought it was impossible for anyone other than a full-blooded Jew, or perhaps a proselyte to Judaism, to become part of God's Kingdom. Moreover, they were so focused on themselves and their Jewish friends that converting Gentiles and reaching the world beyond the borders of their own people group never seemed to cross their minds. Yet when Philip preached, many were saved. So Peter and John, the leaders of the church in Jerusalem, went down to Samaria to check this out. Much to their surprise, when they prayed for the new Samaritan believers, the Holy Spirit miraculously came upon them just as He had come on the disciples in the Upper Room. This was proof perfect that Samaritans could be believers. It helped Peter convince the leaders in Jerusalem that the Samaritan believers were truly in the fold. This was part of the transition from Judaism to Christianity.

The same thing happened in the story that follows. Peter presented the Good News, the Gentiles believed, and the Holy

Spirit came upon them. I can imagine when Peter went back to the leaders in Jerusalem, he said something to this effect, "You guys aren't going to believe this! It's happened again, this time with full-blooded, uncircumcised Gentiles. They not only believed, but also received the same gift of the Holy Spirit we've received . . . with the same signs and power." Actually, his exact words are recorded in Acts 11:1-18. The coming of the Spirit substantiated that Gentiles could, indeed, become Christians.

There's one last occasion when this happens. When Paul first went to Ephesus, he came across some "disciples" who apparently were only following John the Baptist (Acts 19:1). It is arguable these men were not yet believers. Thus, when Paul asked, "Did you receive the Holy Spirit when you believed?" (vs. 2), they had no idea what he was talking about. Paul knew that when people place their faith in Jesus, they automatically receive the Holy Spirit and know it. He may have used this question as a test to see if they were true believers. Obviously, they were not. After they received Jesus as Savior, the Holy Spirit came on them and "they began speaking in tongues and prophesying" (vs. 6) – the same results as for the previous groups.

When you share the Good News of Jesus Christ and people place their faith and trust in Him, they will instantaneously receive the Holy Spirit and they'll know it (Rom. 8:9; 1 Cor. 6:19; Jn. 14:16; 7:37-39; 2 Cor. 6:16; Jude 19). Don't look for extraordinary spiritual gifts such as tongues and prophecy. It is believed by most that these, too, were part of the transition of Acts. Rather, know for certain that when people believe and become part of the family of God, they have all of God, including His Holy Spirit, who now dwells in them.

Crossing Barriers

Philip helped eliminate the barrier against evangelism to non-Jews by going to the Samaritans. His next move was to be obedient to God by speaking to a government official from Ethiopia. No resistance is recorded about the breaking of this barrier. This could be because the eunuch was a devout man who had already embraced Judaism. After all, he went to Jerusalem to worship God (Acts 8:27).

Two racial barriers were down—Samaritans and an Ethiopian proselyte to Judaism. One more barrier remained. To remove that barrier, to convince Jews that full-blooded Gentiles could be saved, something out of the ordinary would be needed. Enter a dream and food.

Dreams make going to sleep an adventure for me. My brain conjures up the craziest scenarios. At times, I've taken to writing them down. One of the more memorable dreams includes food. I was piloting a damaged aircraft over the city of Philadelphia—the engines were clogged and had shutdown; the windshield was smeared by the storm. So, on either Broad or Market, I glided the plane down into a soft and cushy landing. The reason the landing was so smooth, the windshield was smeared, and the engines clogged? Wait for it . . . it was raining baked beans, and the street was filled with the reddish-brown beans several feet deep.

I knew the minute I woke up why I had that dream, at least the part about baked beans. The prior day I had ordered a baked potato for lunch. I loaded it up with butter, sour cream, chili and topped it off with melted cheese. Proudly, I walked back to my table and ate every last morsel. What I didn't realize until later was the bottom-inside of my tie had fallen on top of the goo-ish mixture when I had carried it to the table. When I had sat down, the tie landed on my white shirt, transporting the reds, browns, whites and yellows in a big splash of tie dye.

Well, Peter had a dream, too—more like a vision or a trance. He was on the roof of a friend's house. No, he wasn't precariously clinging to a sloped roof. Houses during this time and in present day Israel are generally one story with a flat roof surrounded by a parapet, short wall, so no one would fall off. Steps or ladders led up to the roofs so they could be utilized for sun-bathing, satellite dishes, and hanging up clothes to dry. The satellite dishes was not a reality back then, but they sure are now.

Their roofs were like our porches. Peter went up to the roof to pray and while there, drifted off into a trance-like state. Before this, however, he got hungry and asked for some food. Perhaps it was the wafting smell of baked chicken or boiled mutton that led his mind into a potential food scenario. We know, after the fact, God was teaching him a great, world-changing lesson.

A Sheet From Heaven

In this vision, Peter saw what appeared to be a sheet. Think "sail" from a sailboat. It was "let down by its four corners upon the earth" (Acts 10:11). The sheet came down and went up three times. This number may have held greater meaning for Peter. Peter betrayed Jesus three times, and he was reinstated by Jesus saying, "Feed my sheep," three times. Peter must have known that thrice, being more than twice, is precise in its meaning, something more than mere advice. It was something he must notice.

The sheet contained animals of all kinds, presumably clean and unclean, along with reptiles and birds. Peter was told to kill the animals and eat them. He refused. Nothing unclean had ever crossed his lips, and he was not about to start now—despite the fact it was God telling him to do so. Peter often challenged Jesus while they were together, as he opened his mouth and inserted his foot, ankle and leg right up to the knee. We could give him credit in this case for sticking to his principles. We should give him more credit for not only listening to God's lesson, but allowing the ingrained barriers to be challenged and acting accordingly.

What did the vision mean?

There are various interpretations—one that is rather farfetched, another that might have some relevance, and a third that is definitely true.

The first interpretation has to do with animals in Heaven. Since the animals are coming down from the heavens, does this mean that animals, including my dog, Muffy, who meant so much to me, is up in Heaven? No. This is not a support passage for "all good dogs go to Heaven." And even if it was, Muffy, who was known to bite people she did not know or like—the gals who checked our electric meter, a policeman, and a dear friend who has a scare on his nose—would not be classified as a "good dog." I'm not suggesting Heaven will be void of animals. But this isn't a proof text for that concept.

Second is the suggestion that the vision was intended to change the Jewish dietary laws. In Mark 7:14-23, Jesus changed the mandate from only certain "clean" animals to any kind of animal. Perhaps Peter's vision reinforced that principle.

The certifiable meaning of the vision involves the relationship between Christian Jews and Gentiles. As already mentioned, Jews and Gentiles did not get along. A famous prayer of a Jewish man was, "Thank God I am not a Gentile, a slave or a woman." Jews felt they were blessed and Gentiles were cursed. Therefore, they would not touch anything belonging to a Gentile. They wouldn't even let one come into their homes. Most certainly, they would not break bread together. And the feelings were mutual. Tragically, this animosity continues to this day, especially between the Jews and their neighbors. One side would like to be left alone (the Jews), while the other has pledged to leave them alone after having drowned them into the Mediterranean Sea. No love lost there!

One of the purposes of the church, however, is to bring the two sides together and become one (Eph. 2:16-18). This vision teaches that since God is no respecter of persons, neither should Peter, the disciples, nor the rest of the Christian Jews. They should not look down on Gentiles. No one should be racially profiled. The church is to be integrated.

Peter got the point, especially when three men showed up at this oceanside villa, (there's that number three again). These fellows, all Gentiles we presume, were sent by a righteous Gentile, a centurion with the Italian Cohort, who was "a devout man who feared God with all his household, gave alms generously to the people, and prayed continually to God" (Acts 10:2). God came to this man, Cornelius, by way of a vision and told him to send for a man by the name of Peter and to listen to whatever message he had for them.

The Same Gift

To make a long story short, Peter went with the men. He met Cornelius, who bowed down in respect to worship Peter. Peter was quick to correct him—"stand up; I too am a man" (Acts 10:26). He was also quick to inform this household of guests that this was not something he would typically do. "You yourselves know how unlawful it is for a Jew to associate with or to visit anyone of another nation." Then he added, "but God has shown me that I should not call any person common or unclean" (vs. 28).

The setting almost sounds like the DeMoss Plan—the witnesses' technique mentioned in the last chapter—the "Set-Up" approach with "Outreach Dinner Parties." Cornelius invites his friends to hear what the preacher, Peter, had to say. After Peter presented the Gospel, the Gentiles were saved and the Holy Spirit came upon them. They were baptized. And Peter, along with a few others he brought as witnesses, testified before the apostles and brothers back in Jerusalem about the ministry to the Gentiles. "If then God gave the same gift to them as He gave to us when we believed in the Lord Jesus Christ, who was I that I could stand in God's way?"(11:17). It's hard to argue against the "God card." The brothers gave God the glory and announced, "Then to the Gentiles also God has granted repentance that leads to life" (11:18). Jesus' command—"You will be my witnesses in Jerusalem and in all Judea and Samaria, and to the end of the earth" (Acts 1:8)—was starting to take shape.

Ever since then the church has been completely integrated without respect of persons and without prejudice or bias of any kind. All churches are open to "red, brown, yellow, black and white." "We are one in the Spirit, we are one in the Lord ." We are a perfect example of unity, the fulfillment of Jesus' prayer in John 17.

NOT!

A Dream that Changed the World

In reality we are one, but in practice . . . well that's another story. Someone has said the most segregated hour in America is from 11 until 12 every Sunday morning.

I understand cultures are different and, thus, the way they worship often varies. Even within the same color communities, worship differs—high church, hymns only, contemporary music, piano and organ alone, full band, no musical instruments at all, old order, KJV only, raising hands, sitting on hands, and so forth. I suppose, to some degree, this is okay. Different strokes for different folks, right? A more sophisticated person might appreciate a certain style as opposed to one with less education. That doesn't mean they are wrong.

The problem lies when groups build walls around their church and themselves to insulate them from the "other kind."

Coming Together

I grew up in a very conservative Christian home during the '60s and '70s with blinders on my eyes. I felt my church, denomination, and a few others had a corner on the market when it came to truth and the Christian way. In my naïveté, other churches, even those of some of my friends, were either misguided, bordered on heresy and liberalism, or were flat-out non-Christian. When I became a pastor, I wanted to fellowship with "my kind." I even attempted to organize a once-a-month pastor's prayer breakfast of "my kind." But when I talked to one brother, he informed me if a certain pastor from town was going to be there, he would not come. The other minister said the same about him. I was stunned! We're part of the same team, I thought. The "same kind." But instead of pursuing it, I dropped it.

Some years later, while at a Pastors' Promise Keepers Rally in Atlanta, Georgia, I ran into a black pastor from my community—Duane Britton, who pastored a charismatic church. He and I, along with another ministering brother, Mark Saunders, vowed we would drop our ecclesiastical predilections, hang our clerical robes in the vestibule and concentrate on a key business of pastors—praying. Every Wednesday morning, at 7 a.m., we gathered at a different church (per month) to pray. All pastors were invited. The initial two from years ago who could not get along had long since moved on - one was out of the ministry. Most of the pastors from the local ministerium did not come. But the local pastors who did, sometimes as many as fifteen or more, saw walls come down. We met just for prayer. No singing (unless a prayer led into something), no preaching, no book reviews, no theological discussions, no gossip, no comparing attendance ... just prayer.

We began to view ourselves as a unit, as the body of Christ, with different outlets or outposts of ministry. We also agreed that together we could accomplish more than as separate entities. So we held a few evangelistic outreaches at the local high school. A key moment came right after the terrorist attacks of September 11, 2001. Since we had prayed and worked together, we knew exactly what needed to be done—hope must be given to those who seemed so hopeless from the shock of it all. They needed to hear that Jesus Christ was still on the throne and He could give them peace despite the turmoil of the present age and events. That Sunday, five days after September 11, we rented the local high school auditorium. The soloist and trumpeter, Bruce Heffner, who was already scheduled for my church that evening, provided the special music. We brought in a pastor who lived in Manhattan and had ridden his bike into ground zero on 9-11 to help minister to people. The service was open to our community. People heard the Gospel and responded. Christians recommitted themselves to the Lord. But it only happened because, as one brother used to pray each time we gathered, "Lord, the church of Ephrata has come together to pray."[2]

The greatest thing that happened to me, personally, was that my theological blinders were removed. I was now able to embrace pastors and churches which had been, of all things, competitors. Instead of division, we became one. Baptist, Independent Bible, United Methodist, Reformed Presbyterian, Grace Brethren, Brethren in Christ, Mennonite, Bible Fellowship,

Evangelical Congregational, Dove Fellowship and others all joined together every Wednesday at 7 a.m. to pray. It still continues to this day.

That, unfortunately, is not the same in many quarters of this world. We are not one. We are divided with our own personal and denominational idiosyncrasies. These keep us apart and keep us from doing the work of the ministry to the fullest. No wonder we struggle in winning the world for Christ. We can't even get along with "our kind," those of like faith. How can we expect to reach out to a dying world?

Casting the Net

But let's cast the net into the secular world. Not only within the church do we struggle to get along and denominations are polarized, but we have a difficult time reaching out to the lost who are of another nationality. It's OK to send missionaries "over there"—people who are called to go to the unreached and have a passion for a particular people. But we are unwilling to cross the street to the Muslim who recently purchased a house on our block, the Jewish shop owner where we get supplies, or the person holding a green card from a far-eastern country who works temporarily at our company.

Yet God, in His sovereign will, has brought these people to our shores and, almost literally, to our doorsteps to hear the Good News. It costs nothing to go to them—other than our "justified" prejudices. These individuals, created in God's image, are like you and me needing Jesus as their Savior. God doesn't despise their color or nationality. He doesn't see it. He sees people He loved so much He sent His Son to die on the cross for them. Therefore, for us not to reach out to them is not only unkind and unloving, it is sin!

Can we cast the net even further as we attempt to challenge our commitment to going to the ends of the earth and following God's heart of loving everyone and not being a respecter of persons? What about that person or couple who has moved onto your street, whose lifestyle is not only anti-Biblical but something you abhor? The very thought of what they do, think, or say gives you the willies. It creeps you out. You not only won't break bread with them, you won't allow them to come into your house for fear they might taint your children or rub off on you instead of you rubbing off on them.

This is all understandable and potentially noble, wanting to protect you and your family. But it does not cut the mustard when it comes to Jesus' commission! This sounds more like the opinion of the early Christian Jews in regard to Gentiles. Gentiles were filthy. They were unclean. Uncircumcised. Their practices were abhorrent to Jews. Why, they even ate pork, the other white meat. They probably smelled, and definitely worshiped other gods. There's no way Jews would want their children to play or socialize with these unclean animals. God's words to Peter, however, challenged and changed them: "What God has made clean, do not call common" (Acts 10:15). Peter's response to the salvation of these once-hated people should be ours. "Truly I understand that God shows no partiality, but in every nation anyone who fears Him and does what is right is acceptable to Him" (Acts. 10:34-35).

We build walls to protect ourselves and our family from outside influences. We tend to cloister ourselves with "our kind" and are determined to let the "reaching out" be done by the professionals—pastors and missionaries. But by doing so, we violate Jesus' command to "make disciples of all nations" (Mt. 28:19).

The purpose of this book is to encourage you to share your faith in a non-confrontational manner—telling others about the Good News of Jesus Christ. The initial emphasis may have weighed too heavily on just reaching out to your friends, your Nathanaels. Certainly, that is important, since God has already placed these people in your life. But let's not limit ourselves to just those of "our kind." We need to make friends outside of our little circle.

We have a tremendous task that has been given to us. God not only wants us to reach out, He's promised to go with us, to "*never leave or forsake us*" (Heb. 13:5). He is the One who will do the saving. All we need to do, if I can quote F. B. Meyer, is "to be willing to be made willing." Whether it is to a foreign soil, across the backyard or to that other office, it matters not who the people are, what they look like, where they are from, how they act, what they think, their politics, what sports team they follow, nor what they drink. It's not our job to determine to whom we should go. It is to go to whomever God brings into our paths.

So don't wait for a dream of different types of animals and tasty meat to motivate you to reach out to others. Rather, pray that God, who holds the divine appointment book, will lead you to His next appointee, whomever He so chooses.

For Further Thought:

"For though I am free from all, I have made myself a servant to all, that I might win more of them. To the Jews I became as a Jew, in order to win Jews. To those under the law I became as one under the law (though not being myself under the law) that I might win those under the law. To those outside the law I became as one outside the law (not being outside the law of God but under the law of Christ) that I might win those outside the law. To the weak I became weak, that I might win the weak. I have become all things to all people, that by all means I might save some. I do it all for the sake of the gospel, that I may share with them in its blessings" (1 Cor. 9:19-23 ESV).

1. How much of the population should you view as candidates to be exposed to Christ?
2. What are some of the interests or skills of those you regularly encounter?
3. How could you learn about their interests or skills so that you

can gain a hearing or join them in their comfort zone?
4. How could an understanding of their interests or skills allow
you to identify needs in their lives and then segue into the gospel?
5. Like a slave, like a Jew, like one under the law, like one not
under the law, like the weak, how can you serve to tell?

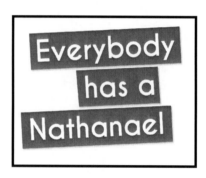

*John 1:43-51—The next day Jesus decided to go to
Galilee. He found Philip and said to him, "Follow me."
Now Philip was from Bethsaida, the city of Andrew and
Peter.* **Philip found Nathanael and said to him, "We
have found him of whom Moses in the Law and also the
prophets wrote, Jesus of Nazareth, the son of Joseph."**
*Nathanael said to him, "Can anything good come out of
Nazareth?" Philip said to him, "Come and see." Jesus
saw Nathanael coming toward him and said of him,
"Behold, an Israelite indeed, in whom there is no
deceit!" Nathanael said to him, "How do you know
me?" Jesus answered him, "Before Philip called you,
when you were under the fig tree, I saw you." Nathanael
answered him, "Rabbi, you are the Son of God! You are
the King of Israel!" Jesus answered him, "Because I said
to you, 'I saw you under the fig tree,' do you believe?
You will see greater things than these." And he said to
him, "Truly, truly, I say to you, you will see heaven
opened, and the angels of God ascending and descending
on the Son of Man."*

8

Your Turn
Like a Relay
Acts 18:1-4; 24-28

P aul had an encounter with the Lord, met Ananias, and went on
to win many to the cause of Christ. Two of them were Aquila
and Priscilla, recent transplants to Corinth and fellow
tentmakers with Paul. When Aquila and Priscilla embraced
Christianity, they became more than secular co-workers. They
were partners in the ministry. After a successful and rather
lengthy time in Corinth, the three of them set sail for Ephesus.
The tentmaking couple stayed there to assist with the church,
while Paul continued his missionary journeys. Then they ran into
a Jew who "just happened" to come to Ephesus. His name was
Apollos, and he was from Alexandria in Egypt.

Leader in the Rough

Alexandria, at that time and for several centuries before, was a
hub of intellectual activity. It's where the Septuagint, the Greek
translation of the Hebrew Scriptures, was translated (second
century B.C.). The city was home to the Musaeum of Alexandria[1],
where great thinkers of the time came to study and lecture. And
it housed the famous Alexandrian Library, which contained
anywhere from 500,000 to 700,000 volumes. The facility also
included lecture halls, meeting rooms and gardens. Built during

the Ptolemaic dynasty in the third century B.C., it was tragically set on fire by Julius Caesar in 48 B.C. Some parts of it survived this fire and several others, but it was completely destroyed during the Muslim conquest of Egypt in A.D. 642.

Luke, the writer of the book of Acts, identifies Apollos as "an eloquent man, competent in the Scriptures" (Acts 18:24). In fact, he was teaching about Jesus in the synagogue at Ephesus when Aquila and Priscilla met him. What he taught about Jesus was accurate. Most likely, it related to Jesus being the Messiah. The problem is he only knew about John's baptism of repentance. I'm supposing he didn't have the rest of the story, the Gospel—the fact that Jesus died for the sins of the world, rose again, and ascended into Heaven, where He sits at the right hand of the Father. Or maybe he did have this information, but wasn't putting two-and-two together. Maybe he didn't know people needed to place their faith and trust in Christ for salvation. After hearing him speak, Priscilla and Aquila took him out for ice cream and "explained to him the way of God more accurately" (vs. 26). Did they have ice cream back then?

Apollos "got it" and became a church leader and preacher. Paul mentioned him several times in his letter to the church at Corinth. When he addressed the division of the church, he identified the various camps: "Each one of you says, 'I follow Paul,' or 'I follow Apollos,' or 'I follow Cephas,' or 'I follow Christ'" (1 Cor. 1:12). A few chapters later, Paul noted his relationship to Apollos in regard to the Gospel: "I planted, Apollos watered, but God gave the growth" (3:6). Clearly Paul considered Apollos a co-worker in the ministry who had risen to prominence. He may have felt inferior to Apollos' rhetorical skills, polished Greek and ability to use the Scriptures. Maybe that's why Paul mentioned he came to Corinth not with "lofty speech or wisdom . . . but only Christ and Him crucified" (1 Cor. 2:1-2). Some believe, based on the high level of Greek that is used in the book of Hebrews, that Apollos is the author. It very well could be. Certainly, Apollos was a major player in the early church.

Your Turn

Passing the Baton

Let's recap: The Lord led Paul to Himself, aided by Ananias in Damascus. Paul led Aquila and Priscilla to the Lord. This husband-and-wife team either led Apollos to the Lord or at least corrected his primitive understanding of what true faith is. Apollos then became so influential in the early church he was listed among Paul, Cephas and Christ. Do you see a trend, a correlation? One person to another person. That person to another person. That person to another person. Winning souls is one person to another to another to another and so on and so on. We'll call it a salvation run or passing the baton.

Here's a salvation run that fascinates me. A Sunday School teacher was concerned about the soul of one of his students. He went to where the lad worked, stocking shelves in a shoe store, and led him to Jesus Christ. The boy's name—Dwight Lyman Moody. Moody became the greatest preacher and evangelist of the second half of the nineteenth century.

While preaching in the British Isles, Moody spoke at a little chapel pastored by a young man. So impressed was he with Moody and the call to evangelize that he left his church and became an evangelist. His name—F. B. Meyer.

While preaching in Northfield, Massachusetts, Meyer gave the following challenge: "If you are not willing to give up everything for Christ, are you willing to be made willing?" A young preacher heard that challenge and was willing. His name —J. Wilbur Chapman. Chapman went on to become one of the most effective evangelists during his era.

One of Chapman's volunteers, who helped set up the evangelistic crusades, was a former major league baseball player. This man, known to party hard, especially with booze, sat down on a Chicago curb after a night of heavy drinking in 1886 and listened while a team from the Pacific Garden Mission sang and gave testimonies. He gave his life to the Lord that evening, eventually taking over as an evangelist for Wilbur Chapman. His name—Billy Sunday. In the early part of the twentieth century,

Sunday was one of the most popular evangelists. One report suggests he led one million souls to Christ.

In 1924, during one of Billy Sunday's crusades in Charlotte, North Carolina, a group of Christians dedicated themselves to reaching their city for the Lord. They later invited an evangelist by the name of Mordecai Ham to come for evangelistic meetings in 1932. During those meetings, a lanky 16-year-old sat in the huge crowd, spellbound by the messages. He felt when the preacher pointed his finger, it was aimed directly at him. He finally went forward one evening to put his trust in Jesus Christ. That teenager's name—Billy Graham. There is no argument on this point: literally millions have come to a saving knowledge of Jesus Christ through the ministry of Billy Graham and his evangelistic association.

And it all started with a Sunday School teacher concerned about a kid in his class who was stocking shelves. Or did it? Who led that Sunday School teacher, by the name of Edward Kimball, to the Lord? And who led that person to the Lord? And so on and so on. A salvation run.[2]

The purpose of this book is to encourage you to get active in your salvation run. Someone led you to Christ. Someone led that person to the Lord. And . . . a long list of people fall in the run before that person—going all the way back to Jesus. Are you going to keep that run going, or does it end with you? I'm not looking to incite guilt. Wait, I think I am. What I am saying is that we've been born to spiritually reproduce. If that were not the case, then we could do as Pastor Tommy Nelson said: "If we are not to win souls, we could baptize people, hold them under and send them to glory."[3]

The Fear That Holds Us Back

God has commissioned us to present the Gospel. So what holds us back? What holds you back? I bet it's fear. Fear of being rejected. Fear of embarrassment. Fear of not being liked anymore. Fear of being labeled a fanatic and ridiculed. Fear of not knowing how to get started. Fear of fumbling words. Fear of not knowing enough. Fear of questions you cannot answer.

According to Jerry Shirley, in a sermon "Overcoming Fear in Witnessing," a survey was given to those attending a training session for a Billy Graham crusade in Detroit. One question asked, "What's your greatest hindrance to witnessing?" Nine percent identified they were too busy to remember to do it. Twenty-eight percent felt they lacked the information necessary to share their faith. Twelve percent admitted they weren't living the Christian life well enough to witness. But a majority, 51 percent, identified their biggest problem as the fear of how the other person would react. My guess is all the rest had fear on their list as well—maybe listed as number two or three.

I could have saved the questioners all the trouble of writing the survey by identifying what my small group said was their number one reason—fear. Frankly, I didn't even need to go to the small group, because that's my reason for not witnessing. My fear keeps me from approaching someone and opening my mouth. It's strong enough to hold me back. It's shrewd enough to argue with me: "You know, they are really busy. They don't have time to speak to you about this. They've probably already heard this. You don't need to tell them. You'll be a bother. This isn't the time or place. Wait for a more realistic opportunity." I could go on. The excuses I create within my head are endless. I always have a ready reason as to why I should not witness to someone.

Here's the Good News. I'm normal. And if you have a fear of witnessing, which I believe you probably do, you are normal as well.

Humorist Dave Berry wrote, "All of us are born with a set of instinctive fears—of falling, of the dark, of lobsters, of falling on lobsters in the dark, or speaking before a Rotary Club, and of the words, 'Some Assembly Required.'" Fears are a natural part of life. But they are exacerbated in witnessing.

Our fear comes from several internal situations. First, we are human and talking to other humans is complicated. Talking to someone who has not granted us permission to speak on this topic, or asked us a leading question, seems abnormal or wrong. Even talking to friends can be hard. We're all humans, and it's difficult to talk to other humans about their spiritual life, even close friends.

A second and even more powerful reason for fear is spiritual warfare. I've mentioned previously that the Evil One is not interested in giving up one of his own. Therefore, he's going to throw in our paths as many roadblocks as possible. One of the most effective is to embellish fears.

Other fears include not knowing enough or not living a life that honors Christ. These fears, however, are our own fault. The recognition that our loved ones might spend eternity separated from God ought to drive us to our knees in repentance and prayer. It should motivate us to memorize a few Scriptures and identify an easy framework or outline on which to hang the witnessing message. (see "Tools for Sharing Your Faith" for outlines)

How to Overcome

As with most problems, the first step to overcoming fear is to admit we have a problem. And we all do, so let's get that out of the way. Repeat after me: "I am scared to death to share my faith with someone!" Do you feel better now? No? Let's move to the second step.

Second, recognize that you are only the tool God chooses to use. You are not a salesperson who has to argue your way through a sales pitch on eternal life. No one is getting saved by you. They are getting saved by and through Jesus. And, if this is His divine appointment, then you are the fortunate one to be used by God—to be His mouthpiece.

"What if I fail?" you ask. You cannot realistically fail in witnessing. I suppose if you were to give out completely wrong information, you would fail. But if the experience doesn't go well, remember God will not allow His Word to return void (Isaiah 55:11). God can use even a poor presentation to draw people to Himself. This doesn't mean we should be lax and give poor presentations. Wisdom demands that we brush up on techniques and verses and words to use. Remember, you plant, someone else waters, but God gives the increase (1 Cor. 3:6,7). Salvation is all on Him. He just wants us to open our mouths and exhale the Gospel of Jesus Christ. True failure in witnessing is not speaking up and sharing your faith.

Your Personal Plan

Third, have a plan. I mentioned in a previous chapter that I like to use a phrase that generally opens the door for further discussion. When someone asks how I am doing, which is a customary greeting in the USA, I always reply, "Better than I deserve." Most people are so used to the typical exchange – "Fine, and you?"—that saying something different throws them for a loop and catches their attention. On occasion they will agree with me just to be nice. "Well, that's nice, I suppose," one said recently. Sometimes, especially when unknowingly I am speaking to believers, they will catch the idea right away and agree with me. I've had precious times getting to know brothers and sisters in the Lord through this means. Many times, to unbelievers, I will get to share why I am better than I deserve.

I've been praying for a particular woman for many years. She owns a small diner my wife and I frequent during vacations. After she went on my prayer list, I happened to learn that an evangelist friend was going to be in that area. I said, "Hey, why don't you drop in and share the Good News with her?" Although he didn't decline, he challenged me, "Why don't you?" At that point in my witnessing career, fear ruled the day. I thought I would pray and send someone else.

Well, today, a few hours before writing this chapter, I had the opportunity to share with this woman why I am better than I deserve. She politely listened as I told her I am a sinner and sin cannot be in the presence of God. Therefore, when I die, I would be separated from God for all eternity. But God sent His Son to die on the cross for my sins. If I got what I deserved, I'd be sent straight to Hell. But because of Jesus and what He did for me, I'm going to Heaven when I die. Then I asked her, "Are you better than you deserve?"

"Why, yes," she nervously said, as she slithered away to go busy herself. By the way she said it and her look, it was obvious I had struck out. She didn't get it, I thought. But did I really strike out? I think not. Maybe I could have explained things a bit more clearly. Maybe, if she had sat at my table I could have slowed down and given her a longer version. A college professor of mine at Liberty University who taught personal evangelism, J. O. Grooms, said it takes at least 45 minutes to lead someone to Christ. In some cases it probably takes more, and others, less. If only I had more time with her . . . then, then . . . wait, I did what I could. I had prayed that God would give me the opportunity. I was obedient to Him. This is now in God's hands, and He is going to do what He is going to do. Who knows, that little talk I had with her might have been the fifth time she's been exposed to the gospel. She's getting closer. Or God, even at this moment, is speaking to her.

I need to be concerned about outcomes but not obsessed by them. I need to hone my skills, and the more I do it the better I become. But the outcome is not dependent on me. It is totally dependent on God.

Having a plan, however, is essential to being a soul-winner.

A lot of Christians do not have a plan because they feel it is too difficult and they don't have the time to memorize something. Well, that's an excuse that doesn't hold water. Of course, it will take time to memorize something. And, yes, memorization takes work—it is difficult. I finally memorized the spiritual armor (Eph. 6:10-18) that I put on in prayer in the morning. I've been praying this prayer about the armor from my prayer journal for years but realized I didn't have the pieces memorized. There are only six pieces, but I still didn't know them. Well, I've got it down now. A little concerted effort will allow anyone to memorize almost anything at any age. Not memorizing something, not having a plan, indicates that you do not take seriously Jesus' command to make disciples (Matt. 28:19). You've basically thrown up your hands and said, "I can't do it," without even trying. That is such an easy win for the Evil One.

Friend, this is serious business! Lives are at stake here. Your loved ones, who may spend a Christless eternity in hell because of their disobedience and sin against God, could very well accuse you for not warning them. Does that sound okay to you? Is that the excuse you plan to give to God when He asks why you weren't obedient to Him? "Um, well, God, I was really busy doing a lot of things—raising a family, doing chores, working, serving in church and I didn't witness because I couldn't remember what to say to people." Yep, that will work! Not!

Evangelist Bill Fay, in his book *Share Jesus Without Fear*, suggests taking a small New Testament, underlining the verses you want to use, then writing the reference for the next verse, upside down, so when the person is done reading the previous verse you can easily turn to the next one. Let me add that you could even write the question or the point of your outline at the same place, upside down.

Trust me, I know it is difficult. I don't mean to make light of this situation. While I was recently counseling a couple toward marriage, I wanted to present the Gospel and brushed up on my *Evangelism Explosion* outline, looking at my "cheat-sheet" cards while driving to the appointment. I had so much stuff in my head that by the time I got to share the outline I was all messed up. I put stuff from point three into point two. It was a mess. I vowed to be better prepared the next time.

Serious business requires serious preparation. In the next section of this book, entitled "Tools for Sharing Your Faith," you will find a number of simple outlines and plans that have been used very successfully by hundreds of thousands of believers. Latch onto one. Memorize it. Use it. Overcoming your fear of witnessing depends on it. Seeing your Nathanael come to know

Christ will make the time and effort worthwhile.

Love Conquers All

Fourth, loving other people will help you conquer your fear. If you really loved someone and saw that he or she was in a dangerous situation, and if you knew that helping that person might put you in that same precarious position, wouldn't you help anyway? The obvious answer is yes. It's human nature to want to protect those we love. So it should be with our spiritual nature as well. We love people. We desire that they will spend eternity with us in Heaven and live to the fullest now. This should be natural for us. It is unnatural not to present to them the way of salvation.

One of the best illustrations I've heard to this point was made by an avowed atheist, Penn Jillette of the Penn and Teller comedy team. Despite disbelieving in God he has a problem with those who do not proselytize. "I don't respect that at all. If you believe that there's a heaven and a hell, and people could be going to hell or not getting eternal life, and you think that it's not really worth telling them this because it would make it socially awkward —how much do you have to hate somebody to not proselytize? How much do you have to hate somebody to believe everlasting life is possible and not tell them that?"

He continued - "I mean, if I believed, beyond the shadow of a doubt, that a truck was coming at you, and you didn't believe that truck was bearing down on you, there is a certain point where I tackle you. And this is more important than that."[4]

He is one hundred percent correct! "How much do you have to hate somebody ..." not to tell them that Jesus died for them and that they can spend all eternity with Him, if they will come to a saving knowledge of Jesus Christ?

Paul told Timothy that God has not given us a spirit of fear "but of power and love and self-control" (2 Tim. 1:7). The Apostle John wrote, "There is no fear in love, but perfect love casts out fear" (1 Jn. 4:18).

Your Turn

If you really love someone, then you should be able to conquer your fear. Many have said, "Courage is not the absence of fear, but the mastering of it." Love should override any fears you have.

Proceed With Prayer

Finally, prayer is an absolute must in overcoming fear. This is spiritual warfare. We're going up against the enemy who is not too thrilled about us trying to snatch away one of his children. The only way we can conquer the fears and the enemy is through prayer.

Did you know that the greatest missionary of all time and perhaps the number one soul winner Christianity has ever known, the Apostle Paul, had fears in this area as well? He who called high priests "whitewashed walls" (Acts 23:3) and testified before kings, standing up for his faith during trials and in front of mobs wanting to kill him struggled with fears. Yep! Listen to what he said to the church at Corinth: "When I came to you brothers . . . I was with you in weakness and in fear and much trembling" (1 Cor. 2:1-3). "Fear and much trembling"—that's me. That was Paul as well. But he did not allow that to stop him from going. He went. When he wrote to the church at Ephesus, he asked them to pray for him that he may open his "mouth boldly to proclaim the mystery of the Gospel" (Eph.6:19). This last reference was written when he was sitting in a Roman prison. Even then, toward the end of his life, he was still afraid and asking for boldness.

We will never be able to remove the fear, but we can overcome it. Prayer helps. God answers prayer, especially when we are willing to be His mouthpiece to share His story about salvation. With God's help we can open our mouth and exhale the Gospel, the hope that is within us.

Katie J. Davis, author of *Kisses from Katie* said, "I am blown away that my God, who could do this all by Himself, would choose to let me be a little part of it."

He has chosen you as well. Through His divine plan, He had someone special conquer fear and share the Good News with you. You received the gift of eternal life. For that person who shared with you, God helped someone else overcome fear and share. Before them, someone else and someone else and someone else. A salvation run—passing the baton. Don't stop the run. It's your turn to pass the baton.

And just think, as David Platt noted: "For the next ten billion years and beyond, that person's life—and the lives of scores of other people he or she encounters in the future—will be completely different as a result of what you or I have the opportunity to say today."[5]

So, who will that person be? Who is your Nathanael?

For Further Thought:

1. How far past or forward can you trace your position in your salvation run?

2. By when can you master an outline for sharing the gospel?

3. On a scale of one to ten, in living a life pleasing to God, where are you?

4. Can God use someone who rates themselves as a "one" to lead another to Him?

5. If you had only one verse memorized that would explain salvation, what would it be and how would you explain the Gospel using that verse?

6. Ask someone close to you for a way you could be a better communicator. And they said. . .?

Conclusion

"Are you a teacher?" asked the server of mid-eastern or southern European descent. He was wearing a dark blue football jersey with the name and number of the New York Giants' quarterback, Eli Manning, across his back. It was Saturday afternoon, football season, and I popped in to Bobby Valentine's Sports Restaurant and Café in Stamford, CT. "I see all the red marks on your paper," he continued.

I happened to be in the area, working on this book and preparing myself for preaching in New York state the next day. "Well," I replied, "not really but sort of. I'm actually writing a book."

"A book, on what?" he asked.

I was had. Somehow I would have to explain to this man, most likely an unbeliever, the identity of this top-secret instructional manual for Christians. "Well," I began, "it's a book to help people share their faith in a non-confrontational, non-offending manner, it's telling the truth as to how someone can go to Heaven."

"Oh, like showing a caveman the light of day by taking him to the entrance of the cave. My dad was into philosophy, meditation and all of that stuff."

"I suppose, but doing so in a non-threatening manner, by not dragging the man to the entrance. For instance, you're wearing a Giants jersey and I'm from Philadelphia."

"An Eagles fan," he interrupted with a bit of playful disdain in his voice.

"Yes, and it's been a pleasure having a Giants fan serving me," I added wryly. After he gave a chuckle, I continued. "But we can raise the level of debate and do so in a civil manner."

"Oh, I get it; we can still debate but nicely. Well, good luck to you," he concluded and then floated back into serving other tables. As I left the place, he was quick to say goodbye and gave me a "see you later."

Conclusion

"Sure, sure," I responded, realizing it was not going to happen. This was a late lunch. I didn't plan to go back that night and I was leaving early the next morning for my preaching gig. Who knows if I will ever get back to this city and eat at this place with him being my server? Worse still, I did not get to share with him the Good News.

Did I fail? Did I blow it? Did I let God down? Absolutely not! The Lord could have opened the door for a longer discussion. He apparently did not. Could that short three-minute exchange lead to something else? I pray that it does. God can use anything.

The key is, we need to "always [be] prepared to make a defense to anyone who asks you for a reason for the hope that is in you" (1 Pet. 3:15). God, then, will use that which we present. He has promised never to allow His Word to return void (Is. 55:11).

In the last part of Peter's exhortation, he utilized two key words that need to flavor our witnessing experience – *gentleness* and *respect*.

It disturbs me that some who present the Good News do so in an offensive manner. They may angrily debate, condemn or speak down to unbelievers in their attempt to win them to Christ— modern day Pharisees. The fact is, they are turning them off and losing them for the Kingdom. They've rearranged the words our Lord spoke to the disciples as He sent them out. Instead of being like "sheep in the midst of wolves . . . wise as serpents and innocent as doves" (Mt. 10:16), they are wolves and serpents who attack innocent doves and sheep.

I had an ongoing Facebook debate with some friends of a nephew of mine from another state over one of the most polarizing and explosive issues of our day. Most who weighed in were high school age or recent graduates. This became quite obvious by their language and immature arguments, as well as their inability to debate without being offensive and profane. My goal was not only to present the truth from God's Word on the issue, but to raise the level of debate and make it civil. I think I

Conclusion

achieved both, especially the last point. One could see their arguments becoming more thoughtful and less condemning, less name-calling. One kid gave me one of the greatest compliments I think I've ever had. When I was signing off, he wrote: "Thanks for not being a _____" (a very derogatory term). He meant it in a positive way.

Gentleness and respect must season every witnessing experience in which we engage. If we have the love of Christ and the joy of the Lord in our heart, and if we are living a life that is pleasing to the Lord and are available for His use, plus if we are preparing ourselves by learning simple witnessing tools, we will be able to naturally share the Good News of Jesus Christ. At some point in our life's journey, we breathed in the fresh, life-changing air of the Gospel of Jesus Christ—the Truth. Now it is time for us to exhale the same as we go to others.

I pray that this little book has encouraged and challenged you to do the same. May the witnessing tools that follow give you the resources to help you present to your Nathanael the greatest story ever told about the greatest Person to ever live concerning the greatest gift ever offered.

Tools for Sharing
Your Faith

One stop shopping makes it much easier when wishing to obtain several items. That's the purpose of this section. All of these tools and many more are available in evangelism books and can be culled from the Internet. However, what's a book touting personal evangelism without actually giving the aids necessary to evangelize?

That was the mistake I made while teaching this material to about 100 Asian pastors and Christian leaders. I was so excited to share the principles in this book within the sessions allotted that I never took the time to give them even one of these tools. At the conclusion of my last presentation, another presenter, an Indian national serving as a missionary in South Africa, informed me that several pastors had spoken to my translator desiring at least something. He planned to present the "Romans Road" to the brothers during his last session. I was rebuked and relieved all at the same time. I made it a point to share some of that which follows at the next pastors' conference.

So, I'm not letting you out of here without offering some Gospel presentations and other methods for sharing your faith.

Before that, you should note the difference between "witnessing" and "evangelism." Although this appears to be mere semantics and is used interchangeably in this book, in particular, and in Christendom, in general, there is a difference between the two words.

A witness is someone who has observed, heard or experienced something about which they will now testify. We witness when we tell what Jesus did for us or when we share who Jesus is based upon Scripture. The Disciples were witnesses of the life and ministry of Jesus Christ.

Evangelism is when we present the Gospel of Jesus Christ. When we fulfill Romans 10:14—telling about Jesus with the intent of leading them to Him, to conversion.

It is not enough to just tell what Christ did for you, you need to implore people to embrace Jesus.

These outlines, evangelistic verses and other tools should help to give you the knowledge that is needed to be able to do this. I've made some comments about a few of the verses, as well as other techniques in regard to witnessing and some organizations about which I have some familiarity. I've also included a completely biased, subjective rating system (one to five stars, five being the best). This is not based on any surveys or factual information. Just my opinion.

Section One - Evangelism Outlines

Rating

ABCs of Salvation ★★★☆☆

This is an outline to use after presenting the Gospel during a sermon or at the conclusion of a fuller presentation of the Gospel.

#1. Acknowledge / Admit that you are a sinner. - "For all have sinned and fall short of the glory of God" (Rom. 3:23).

You've sinned, right? We are born in sin. Because of our sin, we cannot go to Heaven. The fact of the matter is, we will be separated from God for all eternity. "For the wages of sin is death" (Rom. 6:23a). "For the soul that sins will surely die" (Eze. 18:20). So, acknowledge the fact you are a sinner and need a Savior.

#2. Believe on the Lord Jesus Christ - "Believe on the Lord Jesus Christ and you will be saved" (Acts 16:31).

John 3:16 is very clear - "For God so loved the world that He gave His only Son, that whoever believes in Him should not perish but have eternal life." Believe that God sent His Son to die on the cross for your sins. "But God shows His love for us, in that while we were still sinners, Christ died for us" (Rom. 5:8).

What is belief? It is trust in God. Trust in what He said He would do for you. It is having faith in God. Faith is trusting in Christ alone for your salvation.

Do you believe Jesus died for you?

If you do, then #3

#3. Confess Jesus as Lord. - "If you confess with your mouth that Jesus is Lord and believe in your heart that God raised him from the dead, you will be saved. For with the heart one believes and is justified, and with the mouth one confesses and is saved" (Romans 10:9-10).

Confession, in this sense, is more from the heart where belief is found. We believe in our heart and then we confess. It's not speaking about a public confession, although that will often be part of our experience.

Alternative for the letter "**C**"

#3. Call upon the Lord. Receive Jesus by asking Him to be your Savior. "The Lord is near to all who call on him, to all who call on him in truth" (Psa. 145:18). "For everyone who calls on the name of the Lord, will be saved" (Rom. 10:13).

Evangelism Explosion Presentation

Question 1 – Have you come to the place in your spiritual life that you know for sure, if you died today, you would go to Heaven? If you die, do you think you are going to Heaven?
Question 2 – Suppose you were to die and stand before God and He were to ask you, "Why should I let you into Heaven?" What would your response be?
     The goal, according to E.E., is to have the listener identify in what he is putting his hope to get to Heaven. If it is a wrong answer, the presenter will say "Now, let me get this correct, you believe that if you go to church (or a dozen other reasons) you're going to Heaven. Is that correct?" The answer will be used at the end of the presentation if the person, in a condescending way, says, "Well, yeah, I've done that." The presenter will say, "but you said that . . ." So it's important to have them clearly state what they currently believe.

Five Points [Note: For each point of the outline, illustrations are given to assist in the witnessing experience.]

#1. Heaven is a free gift. "But the gift of God is everlasting life through Jesus Christ our Lord" (Rom. 6:23b).
     Because of this, it is not earned or deserved. "For by grace you have been saved through faith. And this is not your own doing; it is the gift of God, not a result of works, so that no one may boast" (Eph. 2:8,9).

#2. Man is a sinner. "For all have sinned and fall short of the glory of God" (Rom. 3:23). "None is righteous, no, not one" (Rom. 3:10).

Because of this, man cannot save himself. In order to save ourselves, we would have to be perfect. "You therefore must be perfect, as your heavenly Father is perfect" (Mt. 5:48). "Whoever keeps the whole law but falls in one point, has become accountable for all of it" (James 2:10). What makes a person a sinner is one sin . . . and it cannot be undone.

#3. However, God is merciful and does not want to punish our sin. God is called a God of love (1 John 4:8). "I have loved you with an everlasting love" (Jer. 31:3).

But the same Bible that calls God the God of love also identifies Him as a just God. "Who will by no means clear the guilty" (Ex. 34:7). "The soul who sins shall die" (Ezekiel 18:14). So we've got a problem. God loves us and wants to give us eternal life, but because of our sin He cannot. He must punish sin.

#4. Jesus Christ

Who He was? The God-Man. "In the beginning was the Word and the Word was with God, and the Word was God, . . . and the Word became flesh and dwelt among us" (John 1:1, 14). Jesus was God and came into this world.

Why? What did He do? He died on the cross to pay the penalty for our sins and rose from the grave purchasing for us a place in Heaven. "All we like sheep have gone astray; we have turned every one to his own way; and the LORD has laid on Him (Jesus Christ) the iniquity of us all" (Isa. 53:6). God hates our sin and must punish it, but because of His love for us, He sent His Son to pay the penalty of our sin (John 3:16).

#5. Faith—Faith is the key that unlocks the door of Heaven. Many people misunderstand faith. They mistake two things for faith:

(1) Mere intellectual assent. Meaning, they believe that Jesus

lived and died. Not sure about the rising again, but if you say so. However, that's all they have - an intellectual knowledge. (2) Temporary faith. They believe in God when they are going through a crisis, but that's about it.

What is "saving" faith? Saving faith is trusting Christ alone for one's salvation. "Believe (trust) in the Lord Jesus, and you will be saved" (Acts 16:31).

Conclusion to the E. E. Presentation:

You have just heard the greatest story ever told about the greatest offer ever made by the greatest person who ever lived – Jesus Christ. Would you like to receive the gift of eternal life?

If the respondent answers in the positive, the presenter will say: "Because this is such an important matter, let's clarify just what this involves. It means, first of all, that you transfer your trust from what you have been doing to what Christ has done for you on the cross. It means, next, that you receive the resurrected, living Christ into your life as Savior. It means further that you receive Jesus Christ into your life as Lord.

If this is what you really want, you can go to God in prayer right now. You can receive His gift of eternal life through Jesus Christ right now."

Four Spiritual Laws

Since the mid-1960s, Bill Bright and Campus Crusade for Christ have promoted the "Four Spiritual Laws" as a witnessing tool. Only God knows how many have responded by following Jesus after hearing or reading this presentation. The tract form has diagrams.

Law 1 – God loves you and offers a wonderful plan for your life (John 3:16, 10:10)

Law 2 – Man is sinful and separated from God. Therefore, he cannot know and experience God's love and plan for his life

(Rom. 3:23, 6:23). [Diagram - arrows shooting toward Heaven from sinful man but not reaching God.]

Law 3 – Jesus Christ is God's only provision for man's sin. Through Him you can know and experience God's love and plan for your life (Rom. 5:8; 1 Cor. 5:3-6; John 14:6). [Diagram – large arrow coming down from God to man with a cross bridging the divide from man to God]

Law 4 – We must individually receive Jesus Christ as Savior and Lord; then we can know and experience God's love and plan for our lives. (John 1:12; Eph. 2:8, 9; John 3:1-8; Rev. 3:20). [Diagram - the left circle has a cross outside, "S" (for self) sitting on the throne, surrounded by discombobulated dots that represent interests which are directed by oneself; the right circle has the cross on the throne and the dots well organized.]

> Suggested Prayer: "Lord Jesus, I need You. Thank You for dying on the cross for my sins. I open the door of my life and receive You as my Savior and Lord. Thank You for forgiving my sins and giving me eternal life. Take control of the throne of my life. Make me the kind of person You want me to be."

"God First" Presentation ★★☆☆☆

Retired evangelism pastor friend, Bob Green, likes a presentation he has created because it starts with God and His perfection and then looks at humans. To follow is the skeleton which he has printed on a four-part business card size (when folded) tract. Bob adds illustrations to each one of the points. Since it is something Bob came up with, it is perfect for him. Not sure others can use it as effectively as he has.

God is Perfect. God loves righteousness; He is just!

Man is not Perfect. "None is righteous, no not one; no one understands God" (Rom. 3:10). "For all have sinned and fall short of the glory of God" (Rom. 3:23).

Everyone has a conscience (conscience means 'with knowledge'). Have you ever told a lie? Have you ever stolen anything? Have you ever had sex out of marriage? Then you're a fornicator. Have ever looked with lust? Jesus equates that with adultery. Have you ever hated someone? Jesus equates that to murder. God will not only judge our actions; He will judge our thoughts! So when you sin, you know it is wrong. You are guilty before God.

If you say that you have not sinned, you make God a liar. God's Word says, if you break one law you are guilty of breaking it all. That means you!

All sinners will be destroyed. Romans 6:23; John 3:3,7.

Jesus Christ, God's Perfect Son. "Christ also suffered once for sins, the righteous for the unrighteous, that He might bring us to God" (1 Peter 3:18). Jesus shed His blood to satisfy God's just demands! You must receive Jesus' righteousness by faith. How?

Repent! Change your mind, agree with God! He hates sin but not the sinner. You are a sinner. You need Jesus to save your soul. ***Believe!*** Jesus died in your place for your sin and was raised to life so you could be forgiven and live forever. ***Confess!*** Jesus Christ is Lord (Rom. 10:9, 10). If you agree, confess to God in faith, "Lord God, I know I am a sinner. I cannot save myself. I believe You sent Jesus Christ to die for me. I confess Jesus is Lord and you raised Him from death to life. I don't deserve such a great gift, but in faith I trust you to forgive my sin and save me from judgment. I thank you for giving me eternal life, in Jesus' name, Amen." 1 John 5:11-13; John 5:24; John 6:37-40.

Romans Road ★★★☆☆

Taking a stroll on the Romans Road has been used by many to present the Gospel. Discovered from the Apostle Paul's writings to the Romans are most of the major points of the Gospel and how one is to receive Christ is clearly defined. It's also relatively easy to remember and allows for logical markings in one's Bible. However, more Scriptures and Biblical principles should be added to it to give a fuller picture. It is a great place to begin.

Romans 3:23—"For all have sinned, and come short of the glory of God."

People need to understand their condition before they can receive the Good News. This plan starts with a stark statement concerning one's plight—that of a sinner. It's pretty difficult to claim that one has not sinned. It's good to have the person admit that he or she is a sinner.

Romans 6:23a—"For the wages of sin is death..."

No one gets out of earth alive. Everyone is going to die. Physical death, which is a result of sin, awaits us all (unless, of course, one leaves via the rapture of the church). But there is an even worse death, one which alienates us from God and will last forever. It is spiritual death. The Bible teaches hell is the destination of all those who reject Jesus Christ. Lost people will live in torment for all eternity. People need to understand that they deserve death for their sin.

Romans 5:8—"But God shows His love for us in that while we were still sinners, Christ died for us."

Here's the start of the Good News. Knowing full well that one's sin will only lead to death (physical and spiritual), God sent His only begotten Son, Jesus Christ, to die on the cross for us. He did what we could not do ourselves. He paid sin's penalty. And He did this not because of anything good about us, but because of His love for us. "While we were still sinners, He died for us." But there is something we must do.

Romans 10:13—"For everyone who calls on the name of the Lord will be saved."

One needs to call on the Lord Jesus Christ. He died for the sins of the world, but, from a human standpoint, it only applies when we confess our sins and receive His gift.

Romans 10:9–10—"If you confess with your mouth that Jesus is Lord, and believe in your heart that God raised him from the dead, you shall be saved. For with the heart one believes and is justified; and with the mouth one confesses and is saved."

The key to these verses is the faith (belief) aspect. It's from the heart, not just head knowledge, that one believes.

Romans 6:23b—"But the free gift of God is eternal life in Christ Jesus our Lord."

Here's the Good News. God's gift (*John 3:16*) is available to all. And when people receive the gift of eternal life, Heaven will one day be their destiny. It must be made clear one does not earn a gift. The gift is offered and received. But the one receiving it must reach out and take it.

Telling What You Know

In his book—*Follow Me: A Call to Die. A Call to Live*, David Plate simply states: "Every follower of Christ knows who God is, what man's ultimate problem is, who Jesus is and what He has done, how someone can be saved and how important it is for people to be saved. So let's incorporate the character of God, the sinfulness of man, the sufficiency of Christ, the necessity of faith, and the urgency of eternity into our everyday day conversations. And as we thread this Good News into the fabric of every interaction we have with people around us, let's pray that God will open eyes to see the tapestry of His glory and believe the gospel of His grace."

The Way of the Master

Four questions are utilized to engage in the conversation. It's an acrostic presentation, to help remember the questions. It's also a slight variation of the popular WWJD (What Would Jesus Do?); instead it is WDJD (What Did Jesus Do?). This is a take off of Mark 16:15 where He commanded His disciples to "go into all the world and proclaim the gospel to the whole creation." Those letters, then, stand for the following questions which can be used in a witnessing conversation:

    W **Would** you consider yourself to be a good person?
    D   **Do** you think you have kept the Ten Commandments?

J On the Day of **Judgment**, if God judges you by the Ten Commandments, will you be innocent or guilty?

D **Destiny**, will you go to heaven or hell?

I have not studied or used this method, so I'm at a disadvantage in critiquing it. One blogger, Joshua Kaufmann, felt it didn't "specifically talk much about what the Gospel actually is. It talks more about the Law and why one needs salvation, but not how to receive it. In essence, it leads people up to the point where they need to hear the Gospel." I'm pretty sure the training *The Way of the Master* gives would clearly explain the Gospel.

Before making a judgment call on this one, one should read Ray Comfort's book by the same name.

Three "Rs" of Salvation

Here's another simplistic approach to presenting the Gospel that's alliterated. My generation and those preceding it grew up with the 3 Rs of education – reading, writing and arithmetic (a spelling teacher's nightmare). So, perhaps, this is an outline one can remember.

R – Recognition of sin and its consequences—Romans 3:23. Because of our sin we deserve death—Romans 6:23. On Judgment Day we will be judged by God. "And just as it is appointed for man to die once, and after that comes judgment" (Heb. 9:27). One cannot save oneself by good works—Titus 3:5.

R – Repentance of sin. This means we acknowledge our sin, and turn to the Lord. Acts 17:30 is a good verse to use here.

R – Receive the Lord Jesus as Savior by faith. "He came to his own, and his own people did not receive him. But to all who did receive him, who believed in his name, he gave the right to become children of God" (John 1:11,12). Believing is receiving.

3 Circles: Life Conversation

Rev. Jimmy Scroggins, lead pastor of First Baptist Church of West Palm Beach, Florida, has developed a witnessing tool he teaches his church and is now being featured by Southern Baptists' North American Mission Board. It utilizes three circles. From a video presentation by Pastor Scroggins comes the following (3 circles are drawn in an inverted pyramid).

In the first (top left) is written **"God's Design."** This is what God has planned for each one of us – for our family, marriage, work, etc. Unfortunately, we depart from God's design (on bridge to second circle, top right, the word **"sin"**). This is a Bible word that describes our condition. It results in **"Brokenness"** (written in the second circle). We search on our own to overcome this feeling of brokenness, doing all sorts of things (arrows going out), but to no success. Brokenness is not a bad thing, for it often leads us to God. The Bible has a word for what needs to be done: **"Repent"** (written on bridge to the bottom circle). The **"Gospel"** (written in the third circle) is the Good News of Jesus Christ. The Good News is then explained (Jesus coming into this world, sinless, dying for our sins, rising again, etc.). We need to believe and repent (the word **"believe"** is written under "repent" on the second bridge). We've tried to change ourselves, without success. That change can only come from Jesus. An amazing thing happens when we take that step and turn from our sins and turn to Jesus. God does a miracle in our hearts. He gives us a new power that allows us to recover and pursue God's design for our life (bridge from last circle to first one). We receive the blessings of God.

The website for this tool makes the following claim, "The Three Circles: Life Conversation Guide helps answer common questions in a simple and memorable way so that you can begin to naturally and actively share it with others." It is easy to remember but requires having something on which to draw the diagram. I believe the website has a downloadable app.

The video presentation doesn't mention Heaven or Hell, and no Scripture is quoted. Perhaps a more expanded presentation would have these.

To watch the video and for more information, including study guides, go to: http://www.namb.net/video/3circlesguide/

Section Two - Evangelism Verses

All Are sinners
~ "For all have sinned and fall short of the glory of God" (Rom. 3:23).
~ "None is righteous (sinless) no not one" (Rom. 3:10).
~ "Whoever keeps the whole law but fails in one point has become accountable for all of it" (James 2:10).
~ "If we say we have no sin, we deceive ourselves" (1 John 1:8).

God Must Punish Sin
~ "For the wages of sin is death" (Rom. 6:23a).
~ "Therefore, just as sin came into the world through one man, and death through sin, and so death spread to all men because all sinned" (Rom. 5:12).
~ "The soul who sins shall die" (Ezekiel 18:20a).
~ "Do not be deceived; God is not mocked, for whatever one sows, that will he also reap" (Gal. 6:7).

Salvation is Only Through Jesus Christ
~ "And there is salvation in no one else, for there is no other name under heaven given among men by which we must be saved" (Acts 4:12).
~ "For God so loved the world that He gave His only Son, that whoever believes in Him, should not perish but have eternal life" (John 3:16).
~ "Whoever believes in the Son has eternal life; whoever does not obey the Son shall not see life, but the wrath of God remains on him" (John 3:36).
~ "I (Jesus) am the door. If anyone enters by me, he will be saved" (John 10:9a).
~ "I (Jesus) am the way, and the truth, and the life. No one comes to the Father, except through Me" (John 14:6).

Salvation Is by Grace (undeserved mercy), not by our Works

~ "For by grace you have been saved through faith. And this is not your own doing; it is the gift of God, not a result of works, so that no one may boast" (Eph. 2:8-9).

~ "Not because of our works but because of His own purpose and grace, which He gave us in Christ Jesus" (2 Tim. 1:9b).

~ "He saved us, not because of works done by us in righteousness, but according to His own mercy" (Titus 3:5a).

You Must Believe on Jesus Christ

~ "that whoever believes in Him should not perish but have eternal life" (John 3:16b).

~ "Jesus said: 'I am the resurrection and the life. Whoever believes in Me, though he die, yet shall he live'" (John 11:25).

~ "Believe in the Lord Jesus and you will be saved" (Acts 16:31a).

~ "If you confess with your mouth that Jesus is Lord and believe in your heart that God raised Him from the dead, you will be saved. For with the heart one believes and is justified, and with the mouth one confesses and is saved" (Rom. 10:9-10).

~ "But to all who did receive Him, who believed in His name, He gave the right to become children of God" (John 1:12).

Receiving Jesus Christ Guarantees Eternal Life in Heaven

~ "For the wages of sin is death, but the free gift of God is eternal life in Christ Jesus our Lord" (Rom. 6:23).

~ "And this is the testimony, that God gave us eternal life, and this life is in His Son" (1 John 5:11).

~ "And everyone who lives and believes in Me (Jesus), shall never die" (John 11:26).

You Can Never Lose Your Salvation

~ "I (Jesus) give them eternal life, and they will never perish, and no one will snatch them out of my hand" (John 10:28).

~ "All that the Father gives Me will come to Me, and whoever comes to Me I will never cast out" (John 6:37).

~ "For I am sure that neither death nor life, nor angels, nor rulers, nor things present nor things to come, nor powers, nor height nor depth, nor anything else in all creation, will be able to separate us from the love of God in Christ Jesus our Lord" (Rom. 8:38-39).

~ "For He (Jesus) has said, 'I will never leave you nor forsake you.'" (Heb. 13:5b).

Questionable/Debatable Evangelism Verses

Romans 10:9–10

"Because, if you confess with your mouth that Jesus is Lord and believe in your heart that God raised him from the dead, you will be saved. For with the heart one believes and is justified, and with the mouth one confesses and is saved."

These two verses play a key role in the Romans Road, the ABCs of Salvation and many other Gospel presentations. Although they are solid verses, especially on belief, the *confess with thy mouth* might create some challenges. What does this mean? Does it mean people are not really saved until they make public confession? Do they have to confess Jesus as "Lord" before or as they are being saved?

Let's look at the "public confession" first. This is not saying salvation is only granted to a person providing they walk an aisle and making a public proclamation or announcement of their confession. Salvation, from a human perspective, happens at the moment one believes (from a divine perspective, it happened before the foundation of the world – Ephesians 1:4). However, confession should be a natural result of this, with baptism playing a key role.

When it comes to *confessing Him as Lord*, I walk a tightrope between my friends who lean toward what has been called "Lordship Salvation" and others who have been labeled as following "Easy Believism." It seems pretty obvious to me, and was certainly clear with the disciples, that when people follow Jesus, He is both their Savior and Lord. No distinction should be made between the two. This does not mean that the new believer instantly stops sinning, becomes perfect and has given everything over to Jesus so that He is Lord in all and every aspect of life. He is Lord, yes indeed, and we are new creatures—"The old has passed away; behold, the new has come" (2 Cor. 5:17). But even the writer of this, the Apostle Paul, struggled doing the things he knew he should do and staying away from those he shouldn't (Rom. 7:7-24).

More study should be done by the reader. When we come to the understanding that sin, our sin, is the reason Jesus died on the cross, repentance (which is a part of faith), should absolutely be an outflow and response to the Gospel message. Sin should be something we abhor and over which we desire to gain the victory. We then begin the sanctification process, which is often a battle between right and wrong, as we conform to live like Jesus and as the Holy Spirit convicts us of sins of commission, omission and evil thoughts.

Revelation 3

"Behold, I stand at the door and knock. If anyone hears my voice and opens the door, I will come in to him and eat with him, and he with me" (vs. 20).

It was a bit discouraging when I learned this verse was not a witnessing one, at least, not in the context of Revelation 3. The imagery of it—Jesus standing at a wooden door knocking—is rich (love the painting by Warner Sallman). But the real struggle came when I realized this verse, and several preceding it, became the defining salvation moment for my dad.

According to dad's testimony, which appeared in *Power* magazine (Vol. 17, N. 3, July, August, September 1959 – "King Football"), God had been working in his life over several months. My mom was missionary-dating (not recommended unless you have the intestinal fortitude to pull the plug if that person does not come to Christ). She was taking dad to Sunday services and our church's camp meeting, Mizpah Grove, Allentown, PA. He was under the sound of the Gospel, especially the preaching of G. F. Yost, Quakertown, PA. Early one morning he could no longer refuse the call of the Lord. What held him back was the conviction that he would have to quit football and become a preacher if he got saved. Only the Holy Spirit could do such calling in one's life—salvation and the pastorate in one fell swoop. Football was his life. Had the Lord not interrupted this, he planned to play professionally (he was invited for a try-out with the New York Giants) and fulfill his dream to become a football coach. But at 4 AM beside his dorm room bed at Muhlenberg College (Allentown, PA) he answered the door and let Jesus in. And this was the verse, along with vss. 15–16, that the Holy Spirit used to convict him and call him to Himself.

He noted in the *Power* magazine—"Folks told me later that this was written to Christians, but to me that night, it was the final blow. I could see I was a sinner, and heaven or hell was my destiny; there was no middle ground."

Placed in the context of Revelation 3 the verse is not speaking to unbelievers. Jesus is addressing a church, the Church in Laodicea, to be exact, that was lukewarm. His plea is that they will open the door allowing Him to enter and become an integral part of their lives.

Tragically, in many quarters, this is the church today—"neither hot nor cold." We are on the verge of Him spitting us out of His mouth. These verses are a clarion call for revival and renewal of the church, in general, and Christians, in particular.

God does use isolated verses to draw people to Himself. However, as ones "rightly dividing the word of truth" (2 Tim. 2:15), using such verses out-of-context should not be our modus operandi.

Section Three - Evangelistic Words/Phrases and Practices

Accept Jesus Into Your Life   ★☆☆☆☆

This phrase has permeated Christendom and evangelistic endeavors for years. Often the evangelist or soul winner will plead with his hearers to "accept Jesus Christ into your life." However, nowhere in the Bible is this phrase used.

After I preached a Gospel message and several responded in a positive fashion, a gentleman challenged me. I thought it was because of the prayer I displayed on the Powerpoint and, thus, I was quickly defensive. I informed him that I was very clear that this was a guideline—nothing mystical about the prayer. If, however, someone from the heart prays that prayer or something like it and receives Jesus . . . He stopped me in my tracks. It wasn't the prayer, it was the song afterwards - "I Have Decided to Follow Jesus." He said, in essence, no one decides to follow Jesus.

Technically, he is correct. Without Jesus calling us, we will not follow. And the same goes for "accepting Him." From a human standpoint, it may appear we are accepting Him. We were accepting the Evil One and all he does, and now we are accepting Jesus. The reality is, from the divine perspective, Jesus is the one who has accepted us. Not because of any good in us, but because of His love for us. David Platt in his book *Follow Me: A Call to Die. A Call to Live* pontificates on this point.

It might sound like splitting theological hairs, but I think the better term is "receiving Jesus as our Savior. At least this has Biblical backing—"But to all who did receive him, who believed in his name, he gave the right to become children of God" (John 1:12).

Profession vs. Possession ★★☆☆☆

"Profession of Faith" was used to identify a person who believed they were a Christian as observed in the following scenario from a church I attended:

At the conclusion of a service and after the invitation was given, a song was sung, announcements were made and cards were handed to the pastor to read about the decisions or reasons folks had come forward during the invitation. For those who walked the aisle for salvation there were shouts of "Amen" from the audience. Some would indicate a desire to be baptized. That would take place before a Sunday evening service. Others came to join the church. There would be no arduous church membership or baptism classes held during Sunday School for a quarter or a meeting with the Membership Committee, rather, they were welcomed into the church immediately. Just by walking up the aisle. Either they came by way of transfer from another church or by a declaration of their faith. The pastor would read "they come by *profession of faith.*" That's about the only way, during such a short encounter, one could identify that they were a follower of Christ. And it seems to be an appropriate way to sum up one's standing with Jesus.

But *profession of faith* may not always indicate a *possession* of Jesus Christ or a true follower of Him. Some folks feel that having walked an aisle, talked with an invitation counselor, prayed a prayer and had their name read from a card is what made them a Christian, as if this was a formula for salvation. It is not.

In his devotional on the Gospel of John, R. C. Sproul noted the difference between the two.[2] From a cursory look, it's rather difficult to know if someone's *profession of faith* is a true *possession* of Jesus Christ. Time will often tell. He then sites—John 8:31-32 where Jesus said: "If you abide in My word, you are My disciples indeed. And you shall know the truth, and the truth shall make you free." Sproul writes: "Do you see the series of links here? Remaining makes you a disciple; by remaining, you know the truth; and by remaining and knowing the truth, you are set free."

The tragedy is that many are the fulfillment of what Jesus said, "Not everyone who *says* to Me, 'Lord, Lord,' shall enter the kingdom of heaven" (Mt. 7:21).

As a Gospel minister I am most concerned about church members and attenders who just make a *profession of faith* and there is no evidence of *possession*.

Walking Down an Aisle to Be Saved ★★☆☆☆

Major city-wide crusades and country evangelists preaching in small churches have often used this technique to invite people to Jesus. So too did Jerry Falwell at Thomas Road Baptist Church and many other churches. In some, it seems like every service ends with an invitation like this. The fact of the matter is, in my dad's tiny church in southwest Philadelphia and as a lad of no more than 5, I walked down that "sawdust trail" (ok, I think it was carpeted) and sat in the front pew where the guest speaker and my dad, sitting on either side of me, reiterated the Gospel and I prayed to ask Jesus in my life.

There is really nothing wrong with using this as a tool, especially in a large gathering and for the purpose of a one-to-one encounter with invitation counselors. The caution is that one does not equate walking an aisle with salvation. There will be many spending eternity separated from God who mistakenly thought that doing this saved them.

And the 57 stanzas of "Just As I Am" has to stop. I know the Lord tugs on people's hearts as He draws them to Himself. And I'm sure someone finally took that step on the 57th stanza (I'm exaggerating), but this, too, can play into the hands of the Evil One as the entire experience becomes more emotional than anything else. For sure, there are emotions involved in receiving Jesus. But logic and faith play a huge role with faith overshadowing all of it.

Section 3 ~ Words, Phrases & Practices

An Evangelism/Sinner's Prayer ★★★★★

The following prayer was inspired by my church evangelist friend, Wendell Calder. As I was moving into more itinerant preaching and evangelism, I felt it would be wise to have a simple, ready prayer that I could share with those who felt called to follow Jesus. Subsequently, at the conclusion of a sermon in which I've presented the Gospel, I pose this prayer, generally on PowerPoint, and with the understanding that the prayer itself does not save. Prayer only expresses what's in the heart. Various individuals have responded by praying this prayer. Brother Calder has seen thousands come to the Lord through his ministry with folks praying this prayer.

Some shy away from any written prayer. I have a good friend who feels that many well-meaning people who have prayed a similar prayer, some when they were very young, think they are saved, but will spend a Christless eternity. The prayer does not save a person. It's not a formula for salvation. Let me be perfectly clear—there is nothing magical about the words of this or any prayer. But Scripture does teach that prayer is appropriate and necessary—"Everyone who calls on the name of the Lord will be saved" (Rom. 10:13; Acts 2:21). It doesn't have to be a scripted prayer like below. Nowhere in Scripture is such a prayer identified.

That being said, for the novice soul winner who would like to have a prayer to share with someone who desires to follow Jesus and isn't sure what to say to God, full well knowing there is no magic in the words, I offer the following:

Dear Lord Jesus, I admit to You that I am a sinner. I have failed You and deserve your judgment. Thank you, Jesus, for dying on the cross for me and my sin and rising from the dead.

Dear Lord Jesus, right now I call upon You to come into my life, forgive my sin and save me. In Jesus' name I pray. Amen.

Section Four - Other Techniques

Better Than I Deserve ★★★☆☆

The phrase "better than I deserve" sums up the righteousness a Christian has in Jesus Christ. If we got what we deserve, because we are sinners, we'd split hell wide open. We deserve nothing but God's punishment and condemnation (Rom. 6:23). However, when Jesus comes into a life, His righteousness is part of the package. His blood "cleanses us of all sins" washing us "whiter than snow" (1 John 1:7, 9; Psalm 51:7). When God sees us, He does not see our sin; rather He sees the blood of Jesus Christ (Rom. 3:25; 5:9; Eph. 1:7).

As a practice, when asked how I am doing, I use the phrase "better than I deserve." This evokes all sorts of responses and typically leads into a witnessing experience.

Because it is often "on the fly" when this happens, little time is afforded to go into much detail (although I've had some lengthy discussions presenting the Gospel). Therefore I suggest you leave a tract. A fuller explanation of being "better than one deserves" is found at www.800followme.com number 250.

"Cold Calling" Witnessing Technique ★★★★☆

Dr. Ron Blue is a former missionary and president of CAM International. Currently he is an adjunct professor with Dallas Theological Seminary in World Missions and Intercultural Studies. He started the Seminary's Spanish D.Min program in Guatemala and has traveled to more than 50 countries. When he travels, he not only speaks at churches, colleges and conferences, but he shares the Good News of Jesus Christ especially with seat mates on an airplane.

When asked to comment on his "cold calling" techniques, he quick-wittedly replied "I don't believe in cold calling evangelism . . . I warm them up first." And here's how he does it.

He begins by asking them about the following:

F – Family
O – Occupation

R – Religious Background

M – Message, present the Gospel

The diagram he draws on a napkin is similar to the one under "One Verse Evangelism." He begins by talking about God, who is perfect. Then he notes that man is a sinner. Man tries to reach God, but cannot. So God reached down to us through Jesus Christ and provided the way for us to reach God.

When he describes faith, he utilizes the very means of transportation they are taking—the plane. "We don't know anything about the pilot, if he is licensed, ever flown before. We take it by faith. And it really doesn't matter what is on the tail (label); it's the plane that gets us there."

One Verse Evangelism   ★★★☆☆

One-Verse Evangelism® is a simple, interactive way to share Christ's love conversationally and visually. It is based on asking questions and sharing truth simply. It's easy to learn because it uses one verse. One-Verse Evangelism® can be shared in 10 or 15 minutes, but can have impact for a lifetime.

Here's a brief look at how it works. Let's say God is leading you to share the Gospel with your Nathanael. Write out Romans 6:23 on a piece of paper or a napkin: "For the wages of sin is death, but the gift of God is eternal life in Christ Jesus our Lord" (NIV). All you need is contained in this single passage. Ask your Nathanael if he/she would like to see a simple diagram based on this verse that will explain God's relationship with mankind (us).

Wages

Circle the word "wages" and ask, "How would you feel if your boss refused to pay you the wages that were due to you?" The answer, of course, is that you would want justice—in this case, the wages you had worked for. Deep down, we all know it is only right we get what we deserve. Similarly, we earn "wages" from God for how we have lived our lives.

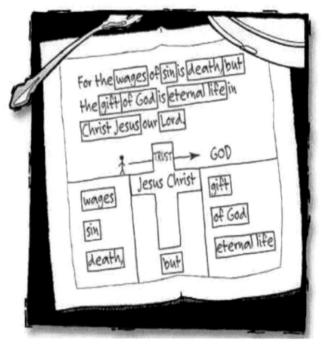

Romans 6:23

Sin

Draw a circle around "sin," asking your Nathanael what he/she thinks when they hear this word. You might explain that sin is more an attitude than an action. It can be either actively fighting God or as simple as excluding Him from our lives. You can ask, "Has God ever seemed far away?" If "Yes," you can explain that that's one of the things sin does—it makes God seem far away. Now draw two opposing cliffs with a gap in between.

Death

Circle this word and ask what thoughts come to mind. Explain that death in the Bible always means some kind of separation—in its most basic sense, separation from life. Because

Section 4 ~ Other Techniques

God is the author of life, a spiritual death simply means separation from Him.
BUT
   While circling this word, mention that it is important because it means that a sharp contrast in ideas is coming. What we have just looked at is the bad news; what comes next is the Good News.
Gift
   Draw a circle around this word. Ask, "If wages are what a person earns, then what is a gift?" Remind your Nathanael that though every gift is free for the person receiving it, someone still has to purchase it.
Of God
   Circle this and explain that the gift you are talking about is free. It is from God Himself. It's so special that no one else can give it. Ask, "How do you feel when someone gives you a special gift?"
Eternal Life
   Circle these two words next, and then ask, "How would you define these words?" Contrast one side of the cliff, death, with the other side, eternal life. Ask, "What is the opposite of separation from God?"
Christ Jesus
   Write these words so they create a bridge between the two cliffs. Help your Nathanael to consider that just as every gift has a unique giver, only Jesus Christ can give the gift of eternal life.
Trust
   Write this word over the bridge you just drew. Explain that a true friend is a friend you can trust, and tell your Nathanael that Jesus is offering to be a true friend to him. All he/she has to do is admit responsible for his sin—either of fighting against God or excluding Him from their life. Trusting Jesus means believing He has power to forgive us for rejecting God and He will wash us clean from all that we have done wrong in life. At this point, you can ask if he/she wants to start a relationship with God that will last forever. If the answer is "Yes," then invite him/her to pray a

short prayer in their own words, asking Jesus to forgive them and make them new.

Close by reminding your Nathanael that this simple illustration shows what God is like: Someone who really cares about people—especially them. Invite them to read all about it in the Bible. The Gospel of John is a great place to start.

Adapted with permission from *One-Verse Evangelism*, © 2000 Randy D. Raysbrook. All rights reserved.

Praying at an Eatery   ★★★☆☆

Many Christians bow to pray before eating. One way of engaging a server is to inform him/her of your impending prayer and ask if they have anything about which you could pray. This can lead into a discussion later about your faith. Leaving a tract is a good follow-up. But, as noted later, make sure you leave a good tip.

Approaches to People About Whom You   ★★★★☆
Are Not Sure of Their Spiritual Condition

Ron Blue has another technique worth noting especially in a church setting. To ascertain the spiritual condition of a person (believer or nonbeliever) he will say: "Tell me how you came to know the Lord." If there is a pause, he then asks: "Or are you somewhere along the path / way?" At this point, if the circumstances seem right, he will share the Good News.

Section Five - Other Tools

Billboards ★★★☆☆

When a billboard is attractive and attention-grabbing, using catchy phrases, short sayings and themes, it can be an effective tool for pre-evangelism. Billboards hover over roads and highways, allowing for the daily viewing of thousands. But it's only a first step. Too much material will make it impossible to read. The goal is for the viewer to write down the phone number, website or church for a later contact.

I called the phone number of an evangelistic billboard and found a live person on the other end. We discussed spiritual things, and if I had spiritual needs, I guess this person might have counseled me. Instead, I was invited to listen to a 15-minute message over the phone. The Holy Spirit may have seekers so convicted of sin and their need of a Savior that they will commit themselves to that amount of time. However, one has to wonder which will expire quicker—the phone battery or their arm from holding the phone.

This pre-evangelistic tool needs a good second step.

800FollowMe.com provides 5- to 7-minute video clips as follow-up where the Gospel is clearly presented.

Distributing Gospels of John and Bibles ★★★☆☆

Mission organizations such as the Pocket Testament League (PTL) feature distributing God's Word. Their boast of great numbers (125 million Gospels and New Testaments) is in reference to the number of copies distributed, not those converted. PTL, founded in 1893, receives testimonies from those who have received their materials. But, as Director Jim West told me, only time and eternity will reveal how many have come to know the Lord through the distributions of God's Word (www.ptl.org).

These groups, like the Gideons who place Bibles in hotels, hospitals, prisons and schools (where they are permitted), are doing a great service getting the Word of God into the hands of people. And a promise has been given that God's Word will not return empty or void (Isaiah 55:11).

At the conclusion of a preaching assignment, I was approached by a disheveled fellow who informed me he had raised enough money to go to New Orleans during Mardi Gras to hand out Gospels of John and tracts. He wasn't sure how many he'd be able to distribute—"until they were all gone," he said. I wondered what percentage of that material would make it from the hand of the revelers to their hotel room and actually be opened. My guess is very little. Much, if not most of that literature, will end up being sucked-up by street cleaning machines early in the morning.

Do people come to faith through this means? Yes. Is it a good return on its investment? Without the personal contact, not as much. It's like the ancient sower going out to his field and indiscriminately throwing seed. Yes, some does find fertile ground and sinks in enough before a bird is able to grab it. Much of it is unable to take root. On the other hand, modern-day agriculture strategically plants the seed at just the right level below the dirt in an already prepared field and spaced out in proper rows. The yield of this crop compared to the other is off the charts. We should follow suit.

Yet, I'd never discourage someone from going and giving. I know the Lord can and has used this method. When all the celebration is done and hangover is eased, a lonely person who is seeking more to live for might just pick up that Gospel of John or Bible or tract in the hotel, read it and follow Jesus. Testimonies prove it.

Distribution of Tracts

Tracts have been an effective tool to present the Gospel of Jesus Christ. What started out as almost tomes (like books) during the Protestant Reformation and 17th century, regained popularity during the Oxford Movement in the 19th century with a series of religious essays known as *Tracts for the Times*. Charles Spurgeon and other clergy published many tracts during the last half of the 19th century.

Spurgeon said the following concerning tracts: "I well remember distributing them in a town in England where tracts had never been distributed before, and going from house to house, and telling in humble language the things of the kingdom of God. ...[Tracts are] adapted to those persons who have but little power and little ability, but nevertheless, wish to do something for Christ. They may not have the tongue of the eloquent, but they may have the hand of the diligent. They cannot stand and preach, but they can stand and distribute here and there these silent preachers..."[3]

In the 20th century, during the sixties and seventies, Bill Bright's *Four Spiritual Laws* and Chick tracts (a cartoon-style presentation) gained popularity.

The American Tract Society, Fellowship Tract League and other non-profit tract publishing companies have printed billions of tracts which have been translated into most languages and distributed around the globe.

When used properly, tracts can have an impact. Indiscriminately distributing them by placing in bathroom stalls, under windshield wipers, in library books, and so forth may not be as effective as some boast. Often they contribute to litter and thus have a negative impact and annoyance.

I've known some who will leave a tract for their server at a restaurant. Unfortunately, a few have been known to skimp on the tip or consider the tract to be the tip. What better tip than presenting to someone the way to have eternal life? This, however, has left such a bad taste in servers' mouths to the point that they shy away from serving Christians, especially those who bow their heads to pray before they eat.

Successful use of tracts is often one-to-one—personally handing a tract to someone with whom you may never have contact again. A ministries professor of mine, the late C. Sumner Wemp, wrote his own tract and handed it to people using that personal touch.

It is important that you choose your tracts wisely. They should have a clear Gospel message. Publishing houses such as:

www.Livingwaters.com
www.Crossway.org/tracts
www.goodnewstracts.org
www.gospeltractsociety.org

have a proven track record in producing quality tracts. Church Evangelist, Wendell Calder, recommends a tract by the Billy Graham Association entitled: "Steps to Peace with God." A packet of 25 tracts can be purchased from:

www.billygrahambookstore.org.

Video tracts by using Youtube, Iamsecond, and 800FollowMe.com might be the wave of the future.

Door-to-Door

Success of door-to-door campaigns depends on the purpose of the visitation. Inviting children to a Daily Vacation Bible School, Day Camp, Five-Day Club or something along these lines can be very effective. It's one of the best advertising means that can be done. As a bonus, it helps Christians overcome some inbred fears. If the flyers being distributed are top quality and there's good interaction with those being visited, it should result in positive outcomes.

Trying to do door-to-door evangelism is much more difficult. The cocooning of the 1990s continues. Gated communities and even towns have laws against solicitation that can jeopardize the program. It is so much more productive if one has an invitation to visit, or a visit can be arranged with someone who has visited the church.

Open Air Evangelism

A sketch board, newsprint, chalk, paint supplies, puppets, rope tricks, flannel graph and anything within reason to grab the attention of passersby is used in urban America in parks, on street corners and in neighborhoods to present the Gospel. In a world filled with video, Internet and cutting-edge technology, one might think this is outdated and borders on tomfoolery. However, the anomaly might be the ticket to catch the attention of folks, especially children, long enough for them to stop, look and listen.

One has to be careful not to preach easy-believism, and follow-up can be a challenge. Training is often available.

Word of Life Fellowship (Scroon Lake, NY) has missionaries designated to work with churches in this type of evangelism and discipleship. Their "purpose is to bring the Gospel to people 'where they are' in public places, where they shop, work, play, and live . . ." The website for Open Air Campaigners is http://www.oacusa.org

Street Evangelism ★☆☆☆☆

There was a day in USA history in which preaching from a soap box on the corner of a busy street backed by a ragtag band of horns, accordions and maybe a drum, proved fruitful in calling people to Jesus. The great evangelist of the 1920s, Billy Sunday (chapter 8), came to know Christ by this means. It does not seem, however, to be an effective tool for evangelism in the twenty-first century.

Times do change and so do methods, but the message never changes!

Unfortunately, there are some who continue using methods that appear to be outdated. Today's tactic is often a man and a megaphone yelling.

Many people are turned off by those who preach hellfire and brimstone. Most nonbelievers will have nothing to do with them, either completely ignoring them or, on the other hand, saluting them with their middle finger and heckling them with profanities while walking by. Unfortunately, too many of these street sermonizers fit the sterotype of condemning and bigoted haters.

Is this an effective way of presenting the Gospel? It doesn't appear to be; however, if a person feels that God has called him to go to the streets, who am I to challenge that person? I'd suggest, however, instead of condemning people, you find ways to engage them in conversation. The constant drumbeat that God hates sinners is not how Jesus represented the Kingdom. Yes, He called out the religious leaders. He, along with the Apostles, went after those in leadership. But you don't see this as the norm or modus operandi of the first century believers. Paul engaged audiences differently as to their needs and what they could handle (see chapter 6).

Calling sin sin is needed in a society that believes the God of love will take them to Heaven no matter what. But can this be done without inflaming people to react in violent ways?

Columnist Sophia Lee in *World* magazine concluded an exposé on these types of preachers ("Men on the Street," Nov. 30, 2013), addressing the ineffectiveness of Christians trying "to force somebody to accept the gospel with their personality, fervor, or rhetoric." But she notes, "The most ineffective way is not to evangelize at all, whether by word or deed."

For an opposing viewpoint, go to the website of Repent America.

www.repentamerica.com/streetpreaching.html

Surveys (Questionnaires)   ★★★☆☆

If it is legal in one's community, door-to-door surveys (questionnaires) might allow for some initial contacts to be made. There are many questions that can be used. This one was used by my son at Grace Bible Church in Las Cruces, NM.

"Hello, my name is _____. I am doing a community survey for (name of church and location). Could I take a few minutes of your time to ask you a few questions that will help us in getting to the know the community better? [It's always good to ask permission before launching in to the questions. It's also wise to inform the person that you are not doing a statistical analysis with this survey. To avoid this, some outreach groups will call this a "questionnaire."]

Section 5 ~ Other Tools

Potential Responses: If the person agrees, proceed to the questions and, upon completion, give the person a packet of information about the church. If "no," thank them for their time and ask if they would like the packet. If no one is home or opens the door, leave a packet hanging on the door handle.

Guidelines: Go in a small group, two, or at the most, three. In *Evangelism Explosion* we went in groups of three with at least one person of the opposite sex. Only one person should do the speaking. The other team member(s) fill out the information on the survey sheet and takes notes. Keep conversation guided by the script and the survey. (Be gracious and not forceful). Always thank the person for their time. Refrain from lengthy visits (unless the Lord leads). Note on the survey sheet those who show a real interest for further follow-up. Be courteous while at the home and walking to and from the street. One's testimony is valuable. No fooling around. Before going out be well groomed; familiar with the script, know what you are going to say, be prayed up and expectant of God's leading. If there are any problems, report them directly to the leader.

Questions:

1. Are you a member of a church? Yes No. If "yes," where:
2. What do you think is the greatest need in this community?
3. Why do you think most people do not attend church?
4. If you were looking for a church in the area what things would you look for?
5. What advice would you give the Pastor of a local church?
6. Is there anything we can do to serve you?
7. Are you interested in more information about our church?

Tattoos, T-Shirts, Symbols ★★☆☆☆

Tattoos with Christian words, Hebrew letters, a cross; T-Shirts with catchy sayings; Cross necklaces, message wristbands, etc. are all potential ways of pre-evangelism. A message is being presented. Hopefully, it is a positive one. Some sayings or images can be very offensive or disturbing to the common observer and do more damage than good. No matter what, the wearer needs to be ready to verbally present the Gospel. It's probably a generational thing with me. I'm not a huge fan.

Videos, Evangelistic-type

Tooting your horn is appropriate if you have a really good horn and can backup the "toot." The people at The Jesus Film Project should be using uber-horns. This project began in the mid-1970's under the auspices of Campus Crusade for Christ and Bill Bright. The film was released in 1979 and has subsequently been seen in every country of the world and translated into hundreds of languages and dialects. What's been called "one of the best-kept secrets in Christian missions" has seen more than 200 million men, women and children worldwide who have indicated they made a decision to follow Jesus after viewing the film.

To put that into perspective, the Jesus Film Project website notes that "every eight seconds, somewhere in the world, another person indicates a decision to follow Christ after watching the *JESUS* film . . . that's 10,800 people per day, 324,000 per month and more than 3.8 million per year!

I would call that an effective witnessing tool. If you come across folks from other nationalities and languages and want to share Christ with them, how about obtaining a copy of the Jesus Film in their language? http://www.jesusfilm.org

Section Six - Organizations

This is a very small sampling of evangelistic organizations.

Alpha Course   ★★☆☆☆

The *Alpha Course* is an interdenominational program that boasts of giving people an opportunity to explore the meaning of life.

It has a simple formula: Everyone is welcome to come eat a meal, hear a talk on the basics of the Christian faith, and engage in a time of discussion. The series typically has 12 sessions, and all necessary material is made available by the *Alpha* organization, including the talks on DVD. Topics range from the person and death of Jesus to the Bible, prayer, and the church.

A missionary friend, who has used this material with some success in a European country, noted that although large changes are discouraged, it can be adapted to fit the perspective of the group presenting it. *Alpha* offers a good way to start conversations with people who are curious about Christianity but not sure where to begin.

The results, seeing people come to faith, are dependent on the presenters since such a wide variety of churches use it (conservative, evangelical, liberal, Roman Catholic, Anglican). It does ask some pretty important questions, the answers to which would determine if a person finds Christ. The fear is, however, if the Gospel is not clearly presented, many may think they are Christians when actually they are just religious.

Since its founding in 1977 within the Anglican church in England, it has become available in 112 different languages, having been used in 169 different countries.

      http://guest.alphausa.org/

Section 6 ~ Evangelistic Organizations

Evangelism Explosion

Evangelism Explosion is a comprehensive church program that enables the soul winner to logically explain the Gospel. This program has been highly successful since the late Dr. D. James Kennedy introduced it back in the late 1960s.

The E. E. program utilizes OJT (On the Job Training). This allows one to learn not only the outline but how to present the Gospel in a somewhat controlled environment. At least it's controlled in that a trainer is with the learners. (See my story in chapter 6).

There are various recommended illustrations for each point. One has to be careful, however, not to come across as too stodgy, robotic or rote in the presentation, thus never deviating from the outline. Another challenge is that questions may take one off the outline and could derail the soul winner.

It is hard to beat this as an organized evangelism program for a church to train Christians in evangelism.

http://evangelismexplosion.org/

EvanTell

Since 1973 and under the direction of founder, Larry Moyer, *EvanTell* has been preparing the upcoming generations to reach the lost by being committed to a clear presentation of the Gospel from a clear handling of the Scriptures with the core doctrine of grace.

EvanTell offers online training, seminars and has great online resources.

www.evantell.org/#sthash.pbmTwdFr.dpbs

Navigators

Navigators, an international, inter-denominational Christian ministry, has been around since the 1930s. Dawson Trotman, the founder, was challenged to take his ministry and make it one which taught discipleship to the many who came forward in the Billy Graham crusades. So it's more of a discipleship ministry, but evangelism plays a huge role in discipleship. We are spiritually born to reproduce. Ergo, a disciple needs to learn how to share his or her faith.

Their vision is to "know Christ and to make Him known." Sounds evangelistic to me!

NavPress is an important part of the discipleship program. It, along with the website, has helpful hints and plans for witnessing.
www.navigators.org/Home

Small Group Bible Studies

A small group Bible Study which has as its sole purpose to make friends and engage in evangelism is an ideal way to share Jesus Christ. Often it will be made up of just one or two believers and five or six of those who have yet to come to a saving knowledge of Jesus. A small group setting is ideal for the seeker to hear and ask questions in a non-threatening atmosphere.

The Way of the Master

A relative newcomer on the block is this non-denominational ministry, whose sole purpose, according to their website, is to "inspire and equip Christians – to teach them how to share the Gospel simply, effectively, biblically . . . the way Jesus did."

Founded by Evangelist and author Ray Comfort and former child actor Kirt Cameron in 2002, this group is concerned with the following statistics: "150,000 people die every 24 hours—most without the Savior, and, as such, will spend eternity separated from God." Tragically, statistics show that as low as 5 percent of Christians share their faith. Their method should help stem the tide.

They believe and preach the Bible is the Word of God, and Jesus Christ is God manifest in the flesh, crucified for the sin of the world, and He rose again on the third day. They believe and teach salvation is by grace, through faith, and not of works.

The Way of the Master is not limited to one method in its approach to evangelism. Radio, television, internet, print media and debates are all used as tools and are well documented on their website.

www.wayofthemaster.com/index.shtml

Weekend Witnessing Seminars

Various evangelists will often hold witnessing seminars at a church over a weekend. Participants will be taught simple evangelistic techniques and how to share their faith.

This is an excellent way, in a short period of time, to train folks within the church. Typically, the presenter will be a good motivator as well.

The drawback is that often there is little follow-up with the participants and, thus, the motivation wears off.

One east coast evangelist who does this is Don Sunshine

www.donsunshine.org/

Endnotes

Chapter 1 ~ Brush with the Greatest

[1] There is more than one calling of Andrew and Peter - this one in *John 1* and again in *Matthew 4*. The first calling was to repentance and for salvation. The second one, and possibly more, were related specifically to becoming Jesus' disciple. John MacArthur identifies as many as five callings for some of the disciples. MacArthur, John. Matthew 1-7, *The John MacArthur New Testament Commentary*, (Chicago: Moody Press, 1985), pp. 114-115.

[2] Both Peter and Paul identified Jesus as – "Jesus of Nazareth" (Acts 2:22, 10:38; 26:9). So did others including: a demon; Pilate on the placard above the cross; the angels who were at the empty tomb; two disciples on the road to Emmaus after the resurrection (Lk. 4:34; Jn. 10:19, Mk. 16:6, Lk. 24:19). Truly, He was "Jesus of Nazareth." But the point is, that was not His birth place.

[3] The Religious scribes knew the true birthplace of the Messiah. When the wise men showed up seeking direction to the newborn King (Mt. 2:2), King Herod called on the clergy to find the location – to assist these travelers, and so that he could recognize Him (yeah, right!). It doesn't appear that it took much research. They knew the birth-place of the Christ-child. "And you, O Bethlehem, in the land of Judah, are by no means least among the rulers of Judah; for from you shall come a ruler who will shepherd my people Israel" (Mt. 2:6).

Later in Jesus' ministry the people and religious leaders knew the Messiah had to come from the line of David. During the Feast of Booths, Jesus quietly entered the city of Jerusalem for His "time had not yet come" (John 7:6). But it wasn't long before He was dazzling the masses with His outstanding teaching while in the Temple. The people were divided. Some thought He was a prophet. Others declared Him as the Christ. But there were those astute in the Scriptures who asked, "Is the Christ to come from Galilee? Has not the Scripture said that the Christ comes from the

offspring of David, and comes from Bethlehem?" (John 7:41-41).
Likewise when Nicodemus spoke up in His defense, the Pharisees
asked - "Are you from Galilee too? Search and see that no
prophet comes from Galilee" (John 7:52).

[4] A Jewish name consisted of both one's name and the father's
name. I would be known as "Dan ben (son of) Russell." My
younger sister would be "Cherene bat (daughter of) Russell."
When I was pastoring in Ephrata, Pennsylvania, calling me "Dan
ben Russell of Ephrata" would have certainly set me apart from
any other Dans in the town.

[5] It seems a bit like splitting theological hairs, but we should be
clear. We often claim "we found Christ" or "we found faith."
Professor and author, Gerald L. Borchert, called this a "self-
centered view of salvation." He further notes, "It was not Jesus
who was lost!" [Cited by John MacArthur, John 1-11, *The John
MacArthur New Testament Commentary*, p. 71). Salvation is
totally of God. He uses humans to present the Good News of
Jesus, but He does the calling and the saving. Martyn Lloyd-Jones
noted, "Nothing is more glorious than the doctrine of the rebirth;
and this is obviously the work of God in us through the Spirit. We
do not give birth to ourselves, we are not reborn because we
believe. We believe because we are reborn."

For context, the entire quote is: "The cardinal error into
which many tend to fall is to think of ourselves as Christians in
terms of our believing and our holding on, instead of looking at
ourselves in the way in which Scripture always presents the
position to us . . . . There has been so much emphasis upon
decision, receiving, yielding, being willing, and giving ourselves
that salvation is regarded almost exclusively in terms of our
activity. . . . Many are in trouble simply because they do not
realize the truth concerning the new birth . . . .[and then the
quote] (D. Martyn Lloyd-Jones, *Exposition of Romans 10*,
www.face-book.com/pages/D-Martyn-Lloyd-Jones/17047056310).

[6] C. H. Spurgeon, "Nathaniel And the Fig Tree," Sermon # 921,
www. spurgeongems.org.

Endnotes

[7] Adapted from Elmer L. Towns, "Evangelism: The Why and How" in *Church Growth State of the Art*, C. Peter Wagner, ed. p. 53.

[8] Scot McKnight, www.outreachmagazine.com/features 5052-is-it-still-evangelism-if-there-are-no words.

[9] C. H. Spurgeon, "The Wailing of Risca," Jeremiah 4:20, Dec. 9, 1860, Sermon #349, www.spurgeon.org/sermons/0349.htm

[10] David Platt, *Follow Me: A Call to Die. A Call to Live*, p. 184.

Chapter 2 ~ Stumped on the Gospel ... No More!

[1] During this stoning of Stephen, Saul, who would become the Apostle Paul after his Damascus Road conversion, played a small role in the execution. He was the wardrobe butler, in charge of watching the garments of those who stoned Stephen. We also learn he "approved of his execution" (Acts 8:1) and then actively became involved in terrorizing believers. It's of interest to see how God used even a negative influence – persecution, to affect change. In this way God dispersed the Christians so that they would fulfill the Great Commission.

[2] The Lord is the One who commanded Philip to go into this deserted place, despite the success he was having with the Samaritans.

[3] According to one source, this may have been Amanitare the queen from A.D. 25-41.

[4] R. Perkins, 2002, http://www.biblicaltheology.com/Research/PerkinsR01.html

[5] His seven-minute explanation of the Gospel can be heard at 800FollowMe.com (#142).

[6] Physical death did not immediately come upon Adam and Eve. In fact, they lived for many years, having a family as they began to populate the earth. Quite frankly, this is the only command humans have actually kept – "be fruitful and multiply" (Gen. 1:28). And men and women have been doing that ever since! As I go over this book another time, I'm sitting in a plane returning from a very productive ministry to pastors and Christian leaders

in India. Despite not knowing this command, the people of India, the second largest populated country in the world with over a billion people, have sure done a good job of keeping it. There are people everywhere!

⁷ http://www.gty.org/resources/questions/QA164 – "What Is Repentance and How Does it Relate to Salvation?"].

⁸ "For I delivered to you as of first importance what I also received: that Christ died for our sins in accordance with the Scriptures, that he was buried, that he was raised on the third day in accordance with the Scriptures, and that he appeared to Cephas, then to the twelve. Then he appeared to more than five hundred brothers at one time, most of whom are still alive, though some have fallen asleep. Then he appeared to James, then to all the apostles. Last of all, as to one untimely born, he appeared also to me" (1 Cor. 15:3-8).

Chapter 3 ~ The Source

¹ Lee Andrew Henderson, http://voices.yahoo.com/six-ways-christians-must-obedient-god-2140482.html - "Six Ways Christians Must Be Obedient to God."

² John MacArthur, *The MacArthur New Testament Commentary: Matthew 16-23*, p. 47.

³ People's NT, bible.cc/matthew/16-24.htm

⁴ God can use and has used others that are not so clean. The apostle Paul, before he became an apostle and follower of Jesus Christ, was actually batting for the other team. He was trying to stop the spread of Christianity by persecuting and even putting to death Christians. In a roundabout way, God used Saul to disperse the disciples and spread the Gospel out from Jerusalem. God can use anything He so desires to spread the Gospel. He can use stones to bear witness to the truth (Mt. 3:9) or animals (Num. 22:28) or angels (Lk. 2:8-15). But in His sovereign design, He has chosen to use you and me – blemishes and all. It makes sense, however, that we strive to be the best possible vessels for Him to use.

Endnotes

Chapter 4 ~ Tapping Into the Source

[1] R. C. Sproul, *John (St. Andrew's Expositional Commentary*, Location 2121.

[2] "How shall we escape if we neglect such a great salvation? It was declared at first by the Lord, and it was attested to us by those who heard, while God also bore witness by signs and wonders and various miracles and by gifts of the Holy Spirit distributed according to his will" (Heb. 2:3-4).

[3] Between Acts 2:41 and this text (Acts 4) the total number could possibly be 8000 or more and this doesn't count women.

[4] Troy Calvert, http://ministry127.com/outreach-discipleship/the-power-of-prayer-in-soulwinning - "The Power of Prayer in Soulwinning."

[5] The "theological continuum concerning salvation" refers to the ongoing debate between Arminianism and Calvinism. The common thread between believers of both views is that what God says is final regarding salvation. Otherwise, there is no reason to pray to Him that He would draw people to Himself or to intervene in people's lives. This debate, however, is of little consequence when it comes to sharing one's faith. God's command is for us to present the Good News. It is our commission. This could be why two of the great 18th century evangelists on opposite ends of that continuum and often in sharp disagreement, George Whitefield and John Wesley, in the end had such great respect for each other and their respective ministries. Its been noted what one of Whitfield's followers (who obviously still held great animosity against Wesley) said to Whitefield, "We won't see John Wesley in heaven, will we?" Whitefield humbly replied "Yes, you're right, we won't see him in heaven. He will be so close to the Throne of God and we will be so far away, that we won't be able to see him!" See "Wesley vs. Whitefield," by J. D. Walsh, http://www.christianitytoday.com/ch/1993/issue38/3834.html.

[6] J.I, Packer, *Evangelism & the Sovereignty of God,* p. 17.

[7] http://www.soulwinning.info/gs/dl_moody/moody-torrey.htm - "Why God Used D. L. Moody" a sermon by R. A. Torrey.

[8] Ron Blue, *Evangelism and Missions: Strategies for Outreach for the Twenty-first Century.*

[9] http://www.rlhymersjr.com/Online_Sermons/2009/080109PM _SoulWinning.html - "Strength for Soul Winning Through Prayer" - R. L. Hymers, Jr. The poem, "Teach Me to Pray" was written by Albert S. Reitz, 1879-1966.

Chapter 5 ~ A Duet that Turns Delightful

[1] John McRay, ww2.faulkner.edu/admin/.../Life%20in%20a% 20Roman%20Prison.docx.

[2] It is believed that Paul's poor eyesight made it impossible for him to write letters. Others were his eyes and wrote for him. This could be why the Apostle put his signature at the end of 2 Thes.3:17 - "This is the sign of genuineness in every letter of mine; it is the way I write."

[3] David Roper, http://ldolphin.org/roper/rejoicing/3043.html - "What Happened to Paul?"

[4] Adam Clarke, *Commentary on the Whole Bible*, from the internet.

[5] http://en.wikipedia.org/wiki/Plague_of_Cyprian

[6] The Jews were supposed to be the light for the world (Isaiah 42:6–7). Unfortunately, they had a difficult time being their own light. They flirted with other lights and gods and, thus, had their light snuffed out. For this new relationship with God, the light of the Gospel and the Christian life, was to shine (Mt. 5:14-16).

Chapter 6 ~ Game On!

[1] http://www.biblegateway.com/resources/commentaries/IVP-NT/Acts/Witness-Athens.

[2] Bill Fay, *Share Jesus Without Fear.*

[3] David Platt, *Follow Me: A Call to Die. A Call to Live*, p. 185.

[4] Yale Center for Faith and Culture Yale Divinity School, David W. Miller, Executive Director Oxford University Press, Nov 15, 2006 – *God at Work : The History and Promise of the Faith at*

Work Movement.
[5] Ibid.
[6] It reminds me of the oft quoted prayer of Scottish Reformer John Knox: "Give me Scotland or I die." When visiting his home in Scotland, now a museum, and reading his quotes, I asked the curator why this prayer wasn't adorning the wall with the rest of them. He responded, "We have no record Knox ever said it." Maybe he never prayed it in public or wrote it, but perhaps a contemporary noted that this was his lifestyle and driving passion.
[7] And now I can add the peace God gives despite losing a 30-year-old son. Admittedly, it has been a struggle. There are terms for those who lose a parent—orphan, and those who lose a spouse—widow or widower, but there is no term for those who lose a child. It's way too unnatural, even when they are an adult child. Much sage advice has been given to us in this regard. One statement which rings true is you never get over this, but by God's grace you will get through it. That is what we are doing. God's grace is sufficient—His peace passes all understanding. Praise the Lord!

Chapter 7 ~ Reach Out

[1] Estimates have the number of laws equaling 613. To see all the laws/regulations and related Scripture - http://www.jewfaq.org/613.htm
[2] This all took place in Ephrata, Pennsylvania, Lancaster County

Chapter 8 ~ Your Turn

[1] http://en.wikipedia.org/wiki/Musaeum. The Musaeum of Alexandria was more than a modern day museum. It was a complex of buildings and gardens containing many rooms. "As a symbol of the wealth and power of Egypt, it employed many scribes to borrow books from around the known world, copy them, and return them. Most of the books were kept as papyrus scrolls, and though it is unknown how many such scrolls were housed at any given time, their combined value was incalculable."

Endnotes

[2] Okay, I admit the "salvation run" from Kimball to Billy Graham is a bit weak. Not everyone in the list got saved as a result of the person mentioned before them. It almost reminds me of the coincidences between two of the USA assassinated Presidents - Lincoln and Kennedy (L elected to Congress in 1846, K – 1946; L elected President in 1860, K – 1960; both wives lost a child while in the White House; Lincoln's secretary, Kennedy, warned him not to go to the theatre. Kennedy's secretary, Lincoln, warned him not to go to Dallas; both successors were named Johnson and born in the same year, 100 years apart ... and on it goes). It will be way cool, however, when we get to Heaven and are able to trace the "salvation run" going before and after us.

[3] Tommy Nelson, message at the 2013 Moody Pastor's Conference.

[4] http://thegospelcoalition.org/blogs/justintaylor/2009/11/17/how-much-do-you-have-to-hate-somebody-to-not-proselytize/

[5] David Platt, *Follow Me: A Call to Die. A Call to Live*, p. 187.

Tools for Sharing Your Faith

[1] David Platt, *Follow Me: A Call to Die. A Call to Live*, p. 184.

[2] R. C. Sproul, *John (St. Andrew's Expositional Commentary)*. John 8:31-59.

[3] www.heartsforthelost.com/evangelism/tract-adventures the-history-of-tracts]

Bibliography

Biblestudytools.com. (n.d.). Accessed Fall 2013. www.biblestudy
tools.com/lexicons/greek/kjv/areopagites.html

Blue, Ronald. (2001). *Evangelism and Missions: Strategies for
Outreach for the Twenty-first Century.* Nashville: Thomas
Nelson.

Blue, Ronald. (Aug. 2013). Evangelist. Interview by author.
Lancaster, PA.

Boice, James M. (1986). *Foundations of the Christian Faith.*
Downers Grove, IL: InterVaristy Press.

Boyce, J. (n.d.). Commentary on Acts 8:14-17. *Working Preacher
Org.* Accessed Fall 2013. www.workingpreacher.org/
preaching.aspx?commentary_id=1536

Brown, T. (n.d.). Understanding holiness. *Tom Brown Ministries.*
Accessed Fall 2013. http://tbm.org/holiness.htm

Calvert, T. (24 Jan 2013). The power of prayer in soul winning.
Ministry127.com. Accessed Fall 2013. http://ministry127.com
/outreach-discipleship/the-power-of-prayer-in-soulwinning

Cecil J. (n.d.). Twenty ways to share your faith. *Liberal Catholic
Sharing.* Accessed Fall 2013. http://liberalcatholic
sharing.blogspot.com/

Clifton, M. K. (23 Feb 2008). Peter's rooftop vision. *the7ones.com.*
Accessed Fall 2013. http://the7ones.com/2008/02/23/
acts-109-16-peters-rooftop-vision/

Cole, S. J. (2006). Lesson 13 - The person God uses. *Bible.org.*
Accessed Fall 2013. http://bible.org/book/export/html/21916

Collins, M. G. (Jan-Feb 2010). The miracles of Jesus Christ: Two
demon-possessed men healed. *Forerunner.* Accessed Fall 2013.
//www.cgg.org/index.cfm/fuseaction/Library.sr/CT/bs/k/1481/

Conquering the fear in evangelism (n.d.). Accessed Fall 2013.
http://mommyevangelism.org/2013/04/17/conquering-the-fear-in-
evangelism/

Did Jesus break Jewish law? (n.d.) *Yahoo Answers.* Accessed Fall
2013. http://answers.yahoo.com/
question/index?qid=20091028113733AA89xyf

Earlychurch.com (n.d.) Love without condition. Accessed Fall 2013.
http://www.earlychurch.com/unconditional-love.php

Evantell.org (n.d.). How to overcome fear in evangelism: Initial
Steps. Accessed Fall 2013. http://evantell.org/Tools/
Article-Detail/Article/10/How-to-Overcome-Fear-in-Evangelism-
Initial-Steps

Ewell, W. A. (1984). *Evangelical Dictionary of Theology.* Grand
Rapids: Baker Book House.

Bibliography

Fay, W. and L. E. Shepherd. (1999). *Share Jesus Without Fear.* Nashville: Broadman & Holman Publishers.

Fairchild, M. (n.d.). Obedience to God. About.com. Accessed Fall 2013. http://christianity.about.com/od/whatdoesthebiblesay/a/Obedience-To-God.htm

Foster, E. (13 June 2012). The social context of Apollo from Alexandria. *Yahoo Voices.* Accessed Fall 2013. http://voices.yahoo.com/the-social-context-apollos-alexandria-11444192.html?cat=37

Fraser, B. (n.d.). Prisons in Paul's world. Accessed Fall 2013. http://www.mpumc.org/uploads/file/Prisons%20in%20Paul.pdf

Garman, J. R. (n.d.). Seventy successful soul winning suggestions. *American Rehabilitation Ministries.* Accessed fall 2013. http://www.arm.org/seventy.htm

Graham, B. (1989). *Choose ye this day.* Sermon preached at International Conference for Itinerant Evangelists. Amsterdam.

Gospel Tract Society. (n.d.). History. Accessed Fall 2013. http://www.gospeltractsociety.org/history/

Gotquestions.org. (n.d.). Is handing out gospel tracts a good evangelism method? Accessed Fall 2013. www.gotquestions.org/gospel-tracts.html

Gotquestions.org (n.d.). What does the Bible say about demon possession / demonic possession? Accessed Fall 2013. http://www.gotquestions.org/demon-possession.html

Gotquestions.org (n.d.). What is repentance and is it necessary for salvation? Accessed Fall 2013. www.gotquestions.org/repentance.html

Gotquestions.org (n.d.). When / How do we receive the Holy Spirit? Accessed Fall 2013. http://www.gotquestions.org/receive-Holy-Spirit.html

Guzik, D. (2012) Acts 10 – Cornelius, Peter, and the conversion of Gentiles. *Enduringword.com.* Accessed Fall 2013. http://www.enduringword.com/commentaries/4410.htm

Hart, J. F. (12 Dec 2007). Why confess Christ? The use and abuse of Romans 10:9, 10. *Bible.org.* Accessed Fall 2013. https://bible.org/article/why-confess-christ-use-and-abuse-romans-109-10

Henderson, L. A. (10 Nov 2008) Six ways Christians must be obedient to God. Accessed Fall 2013. http://voices.yahoo.com/six-ways-christians-must-obedient-god-2140482.html

Herrick, G. (6 July 2014). The conversion of the Samaritans in Acts 8:14-17 and the unified progress of the Gospel in the book of Acts. *Bible.org.* Accessed Fall 2013. bible.org/article/conversion-samaritans-acts-814-17-and-unified-progress-gospel-book-acts

Bibliography

Hoffman, F. L. (n.d.). The true meaning of the vision of the animals in the sheet. Accessed Fall 2013 www.all-creatures.org/d iscuss/svtacts10.1-11.18-flh.html

Hybels, B. and M. Mittelberg. (1994). *Becoming a Contagious Christian*. Grand Rapids: Zondervan.

Hymers, Jr. R. L. (1 Aug 2009). Strength for soul winning through prayer. Accessed Fall 2013. http://www.rlhymersjr.com/ Online_Sermons/2009/080109PM_SoulWinning.html

Ichthus (n.d.). What happened to the 12 disciples of Jesus? Accessed Fall 2013. http://www.ichthus.info/Disciples/intro.html

IVP New Testament Commentary. (n.d.). Peter's Vision. *Biblegateway.com*. Accessed Fall 2013. http://www.biblegate way.com/resources/commentaries/IVP-NT/Acts/Peters-Vision

IVP New Testament Commentary. (n.d.). Philip and the Ethiopian eunuch. *Biblegateway.com*. Accessed Fall 2013. www.biblegateway.com/resources/commentaries/IVP-NT/Acts/P hilip-Ethiopian-Eunuch

IVP New Testament Commentary. (n.d.). Samaria responds to the Gospel. *Biblegateway.com*. Accessed Fall 2013. www.biblegateway.com/resources/commentaries/IVP-NT/Acts/S amaria-Responds-Gospel

IVP New Testament Commentary. (n.d.). Witness at Athens. *Biblegateway.com*. Accessed Fall 2013. www.biblegateway.com/resources/commentaries/IVP-NT/Acts/ Witness-Athens

JesusCentral.com. (n.d.). Purpose of Jesus' miracles. Accessed Fall 2013.www.jesuscentral.com/ja/purpose-of-jesus-miracles-faq.ht ml

Kanaley, Reid. (16 June 1986). Demoss rites draw evangelical leaders. *Philly.com*. Accessed Fall 2013. http://articles.philly. com/1986-06-16/news/26045434_1_leighton-ford-evangelical-ch ristian-leaders-memorial-service

Kaufmann, J. (1 June 2011). Way of the Master. Accessed Fall 2013. http://beansricegod.com/2011/06/way-of-the-master/

Kifer, J. (n.d.) *Phillip - deacon & evangelist*. Accessed Fall 2013. http://justus.anglican.org/resources/bio/264.html

Landis, D. (19 Dec 2007). Christ's obedience to the authority of God. *Answers Magazine*. Accessed fall 2013. www.answersingenesis.org/articles/am/v3/n1/christ-obedience

Lectionary Bible Studies and Sermons (n.d.). They received the Holy Spirit - Acts 8:14-25. Accessed Fall 2013. www.lectionarystudies.com/epiphany1cae.html

Lumpkin, C. R. (19 Jan 1978). Miracles and healings. *Truth Magazine,* XXII: 3, pp.60-61. Accessed Fall 2013. www.truthmagazine.com/archives/volume22/TM022032.html

Bibliography

MacArthur, Jr. J. (27 Jan 1974). From Judaism to Jesus, Part 3: Have you received the Holy Spirit? *Grace to You.* www.gty.org/resources/sermons/1770/from-judaism-to-jesus-part-3-have-you-received-the-holy-spirit

MacArthur, Jr. J. (n.d.). Salvation reaches out. *Grace to You.* Accessed Fall 2013. www.gty.org/resources/study-guides/40-5122/

MacArthur, Jr. J. (2011). *Saved Without a Doubt.* Colorado Spring: David C. Cook.

MacArthur, Jr. J.(1988). *The MacArthur New Testament Commentary* (Matthew 1-7). Chicago: Moody.

MacArthur, Jr. J. (1988). *The MacArthur New Testament Commentary* (Matthew 16-23). Chicago: Moody.

MacArthur, Jr. J. (2006). *The MacArthur New Testament Commentary* (John 1-11). Chicago: Moody.

MacArthur, Jr. J. (2013). What is repentance and how does it relate to salvation? *Grace to You.* Accessed Fall 2013. www.gty.org/resources/questions/QA163

Master's Prayer Network. (12 April 2006). Silas, a chief man among brethren. Accessed Fall 2013. www.mpnhome.net/characters/silas.htm

McCloskey, M. (1986). *Tell it Often - Tell it Well.* San Bernardino: Here's Life Publishers.

McRaney, Jr. W. (2003). *The Art of Personal Evangelism.* Nashville: B&H Publishing Group.

McRaney, Jr. W. (n.d.) 5 ways to overcome the fears of witnessing. *Churchleaders.com.* Accessed Fall 2013. www.churchleaders.com/outreach-missions/outreach-missions-how-tos/146393-5-ways-to-overcome-a-fear-of-witnessing.html

McRay, J., ww2.faulkner.edu/admin/.../Life%20in%20a%20Roman%20**Prison**.docx

Merriam-Webster's Dictionary. unabridged.merriam-webster.com/unabridged

Miller, D. W. (2006). *God at Work: The History and Promise of the Faith at Work Movement.* Oxford University Press.

Monergism. (2009). How to witness effectively. Accessed Fall 2013. www.morningstarranch.org/lesson15.html

Monergism. (2009). What is the gospel? Accessed Fall 2013. www.monergism.com/thethreshold/articles/onsite/qna/whatisgospel.html

Mount Olive Lutheran Church Missouri Synod. (n.d.). Seven styles of faith sharing. Accessed Fall 2013. www.mountolivelcms.org/resources/WITNESSING%20METHODS.pdf

Nixdorf, O. (n.d.). Conquering fear. *Sermon Org.* Accessed Fall 2013. http://www.sermons.org/sermons/sermon4.html

Bibliography

O'Reilly, B and M. Dugald. (2013). *Killing Jesus*. New York: Henry Hold and Company.

Packer, J. I. (1961). *Evangelism & The Sovereignty of God*. Downers Grove, IL: InterVaristy Press.

Peckham, C. N. (n.d.). Prayer in soul-winning. *Sermon Index Net*. Accessed Fall 2013. www.sermonindex.net/modules/articles/index.php?view=article&aid=20393

People's New Testament. Accessed Fall 2013. www.bible.cc/matthew/16-24.htm.

Piper, J. (19 May 1991). What does it mean to receive the Holy Spirit. *Desiring God Ministries*. Accessed Fall 2013. www.desiringgod.org/resource-library/sermons/what-does-it-mean-to-receive-the-holy-spirit

Piper, J (20 Oct 1991). What God has cleansed do not call common. *Desiring God Ministries*. Accessed Fall 2013. http://ru.desiringgod.org/resource-library/sermons/what-god-has-cleansed-do-not-call-common?lang=en

Platt, D. (2013). *Follow Me: A Call to Die. A Call to Live*. Carol Stream, IL: Tyndale House Publishers.

Prayer New England Ministries (n.d.). Soul winning through intercession. Accessed Fall 2013. http://www.prayernewengland.org/soul-winning-through-intercession/

Pritchard, R. (Nov. 2013). Sermon heard at Word of Life Church Leadership Conference. Schroon Lake, NY.

Quinn, J. W. (7 July 2000). He is both Lord and Christ. *Expository Files*. Accessed Fall 2013. www.bible.ca/ef/expository-romans-10-9-10.htm

Reid, W. C. (n.d.). The church at Ephesus. *Stem Publishing*. Accessed Fall 2013. www.stempublishing.com/magazines/OSW/51-60/osw52b.html

Rich, T. (2011). A list of 613 Mitzvot (commandments). *Jewfaq.org*. Accessed Fall 2013. http://www.jewfaq.org/613.htm

Richards, L. O. (1985). *Expository Dictionary of Bible Words*. Grand Rapids: Zondervan Publishing House.

Rober, D. H. (10 Sept. 1972). What happened to Paul? *Discovery Publishing*. Accessed Fall 2013. http://ldolphin.org/roper/rejoicing/3043.html

Saini, Jessica. (n.d.) How many gods are there in India? *Wiki.answers*. Accessed Fall 2013. http://wiki.answers.com/Q/How_many_gods_are_there_in_india#slide1

Selassie, S. H. (Dec 1970). The establishment of the Ethiopian church. *Ethiopianorthodox.org*. Accessed Fall 2013. www.ethiopianorthodox.org/english/ethiopian/prechristian.html

Bibliography

Sedler, M. D. (2003). *When to Speak Up and When to Shut Up*. Grand Rapids, MI: Baker Publishing Group.

Septuagint Net (n.d.). Septuagint and reliability. http://www.septuagint.net/

Sharing Jesus Blogspot (15 October 2006). The effectiveness and history of Gospel tract distribution. Accessed Fall 2013. http://sharingjesus.blogspot.in/2006/10/effectiveness-and-history-of-gospel.html

Shelhamer, E. E. (n.d.). Steps in seeking holiness. *Ochristian.com*. Accessed Fall 2013. articles.ochristian.com/article13272.shtml

Shirley, J. (n.d.). Overcoming fear in witnessing. *SermonCentral*. Accessed Fall 2013. www.sermoncentral.com/sermons/overcoming-fear-in-witnessing-jerry-shirley-sermon-on-sharing-your-faith-67872.asp

Smith. M. W. (2010). Christians stood out in early Christianity for their love to all during terrifying epidemics while others fled. *Original Christianity Net*. Accessed Fall 2013. http://www.originalchristianity.net/?p=2333

Sobczak, A. (2010). *Smart Calling*. Hoboken, NJ: John Wiley & Sons, Inc.

Sproul, R. C. *John (St. Andrew's Expositional Commentary)*. Ann Arbor, MI: Sheridan Books, Inc. 2009.

Spurgeon, C. H. (n.d.). The soul winner's life and work. *Spurgeon.com*. Accessed Fall 2013. www.spurgeon.org/misc/sw11.htm

Stanley, C. (2013). Obedience leads to blessing. *In Touch Ministries*. Accessed Fall 2013. www.intouch.org/you/bible-studies/content/topic/obedience_leads_to_blessing

Stanton, G. T. (10 July 2012). FactChecker: Misquoting Francis Assisi. *The Gospel Coalition*. Accessed Fall 2013. http://thegospelcoalition.org/blogs/tgc/2012/07/11/factchecker-misquoting-francis-of-assisi/

Steve (10 July 2011). Who was Apollos? *Christianhistory101.com*. Accessed Fall 2013. www.churchhistory101.com/feedback/paul-apollos-hebrews.php

The Open Scroll (n.d.). Peter's vision of the Gentile age. Accessed Fall 2013. www.theopenscroll.com/beyond_veil/petersvision.htm

Torrey, R. A. (1923). Why God used D. L. Moody. *Sword of the Lord Publishers*. Accessed Fall 2013. www.soulwinning.info/gs/dl_moody/moody-torrey.htm

Towns, E. L. (1988). *Evangelism: The Why and How*. Wheaton: Tyndale.

Tozer, A. W. (n.d.). Jesus a model soul winner. *Where God Builds Disciples*. Accessed Fall 2013. www.wgbd.org/tozersoul.html

Bibliography

Truth Net Org (n.d.). The Holy Spirit indwelling the believer. Accessed Fall 2013.
www.truthnet.org/Holy-Spirit/5HolySpirit-Indwelling

Upon the Solid Rock (n.d.). Edward Kimball - the legacy of a Sunday School teacher. Accessed Fall 2013.
http://uponthesolidrock.wordpress.com/2010/12/05/edward-kimb all-the-legacy-of-a-sunday-school-teacher/

Van Biema, D. (1 Aug 1999). Who are these guys? *Time*. Accessed fall 2013.
content.time.com/time/magazine/article/0,9171,28859,00

Walsh, J. D. (1 April 1993). Wesley vs. Whitefield. *Christian History*. Accessed Fall 2013.
http://www.christianitytoday.com/ch/1993/issue38/3834.html

Whyte, III. D. (n.d.). The soul-winning motivator. Accessed Fall 2013. http://soulwinningmotivator.buzzsprout.com/

Wikipedia.org (2013). Areopagus. Accessed Fall 2013.
http://en.wikipedia.org/wiki/Areopagus

Wikipedia.org (2013). Eunuch. Accessed Fall 2013.
http://en.wikipedia.org/wiki/Eunuch

Wikipedia.org (2013). Hindu gods. Accessed Fall 2013.
http://en.wikipedia.org/wiki/God_in_Hinduism

Wikipedia.org (2013). Library of Alexandria. Accessed Fall 2013.
http://en.wikipedia.org/wiki/Library_of_Alexandria

Wikipedia.org (2013). Tracts. Accessed Fall 2013.
http://en.wikipedia.org/wiki/Tract_(literature)

Biography of Author

Dan Allen, born in Quakertown, PA on July 8, 1955, was born again at an early age in his dad's church in Philadelphia. He was raised in a minister's home, which gave him a bird's-eye view of the profession to which he would later be called. It also afforded plenty of opportunities to assist his dad in the ministry. As a teenager, college student, and seminarian, he taught Sunday School, led Junior Church, led worship, directed the bus ministry, worked in the media ministry of the church and preached.

He is a graduate of Liberty University, Lynchburg, VA, with a B.S. in Pastoral Ministries; M.A. in Religious Thought from Biblical Theological Seminary, Hatfield, PA; D.D. Lancaster Bible College, Lancaster, PA.

His first charge was at Faith Fellowship Chapel in Cape May Court House, NJ in 1979 (now Cape Community Church). Two years later he joined the staff of the Bible Fellowship Church of Ephrata as Pastor of Education, and in 1982 became the Senior Pastor until December 31, 2004.

During both pastorates, the Lord opened many doors of service especially in the area of media. He continues a radio ministry entitled "Minute Meditations." These minute spots have been aired on various stations in Pennsylvania, Maryland and Colorado. His most recent 1-minute message series "Proclaiming the Passion," is aired during Passion Week in several additional states as well as on Trans World Radio stations from Bonaire (for South America) and South Africa. His first venture in television was a debate format on a local cable entitled: *Public Pulpit*. He sat in the conservative chair pitted against a liberal pastor. This aired for five years. For six years he produced a program called **the bottomline**—a half-hour program aired in south-central Pennsylvania and Maryland. On this program he discussed contemporary topics from a Biblical, moral, and ethical perspective and always concluded by giving "the bottom line." He has also been featured in Christian Public Service announcements. He writes letters to various newspapers espousing conservative, Christian views. He has done some freelance writing, submitting articles to several newspapers. He is outspoken on various moral and biblical issues. For a number of years he has been writing an article for SAGE—a monthly insert for seniors in the *Pocono Record* located in Stroudsburg, PA. He has also spoken at Christian Conference centers and Christian schools.

From January 2005 until November 2011 he was the Director of Pinebrook Bible Conference. His goal was to carry on the work that Pinebrook's founder, Percy Crawford, so adequately established at Pinebrook by providing one of the best spiritual retreats on the Mid-Atlantic Coast.

Dan has won awards including Who's Who in American Colleges and Universities and Outstanding Young Men of America. He is a member of the National Religious Broadcasters.

He has served on various committees and agencies of the Bible Fellowship Church denomination and has had other responsibilities of leadership. He has been an advisory member of Lancaster County ACTION (a Christian political action committee) and was on the boards of Christian Counseling of Lancaster County and Life Change Ministries, Int. He is also a member of the Lancaster Bible College Corporation Board.

In 2003 Dan went on his first mission trip to India to preach and teach pastors and Christian leaders. Subsequently he has worked with BCM International, Hope & Help International, India Village Ministries and TEAM-India (all in India). He has preached in a number of village churches as well as large, established churches on both coasts and in central India. One sermon had him preaching to several thousand . . . a number of which became followers of Jesus. His desire, however, is to help church leaders especially in this South Asian country.

In the Spring of 2012 Dan accepted an offer to start an evangelism ministry using an 800-number and the web – encouraging, equipping and enabling Christians, churches and Christian media in evangelism. Under the 800FollowMe banner is "The Nathanael Project"—a two month church-evangelism program for the entire church. (See ad on page 184)

In February 2013, Dan restarted *Joy in Jesus Ministries*. Initially birthed to assist in his media ministry in 1993, it remained dormant for twenty years. This personal 501c3 ministry of Dan and Vonnie Allen, under the direction of a Board of Directors, seeks to mentor ministers/wives; reach out to the Christian community through media and messages; and to continue his mission to India. Dan and Vonnie are presently missionaries associates with the Bible Fellowship Church Board of Missions.

Each Sunday Dan represents **800FollowMe.com**, *Joy in Jesus Ministries*, and his Lord as he preaches at various churches. He'd love to come to your church, camp, school or ministry! You can reach Dan dan@800followme.com

Dan is married to the former Vonnette E. Day of Colorado Springs, Colorado, and they have three married children and seven-grandchildren (whose photos he'd gladly share!) and one son who is with the Lord.

Pastor Dan is driven by the reality that many folks do not know Jesus as their personal Lord and Savior. He wants everyone to experience the same joy he has found in Jesus Christ. Thus, he wishes all "Joy in Jesus."

Short Biography of Dr. Elmer Towns

Dr. Elmer Towns is co-founder of the largest, private non-profit university in the world - Liberty University, Lynchburg, VA. Along with Jerry Falwell the school was started in 1971 with the pledge of training young champions for Christ. At the university, Towns has been dean of the B. R. Lakin School of Religion, Liberty Baptist Theological Seminary, and Distinguished Professor of Systematic Theology. Towns has authored over 170 books many of which focus on the church - church growth, church leadership, Christian education, Sunday School, as well as books on prayer and fasting.

Appreciation

I've dedicated this book to two very important people in my life. First is my father, about whom I speak in the introduction. I was his son, he was my dad, my pastor, my mentor and my friend. His loss, while I was at my first church, was a huge blow to a 24-year-old budding preacher. But God used his passing to strengthen and force me to depend more heavily on my Heavenly Father so that I would be found an acceptable and faithful under-shepherd. I still need to depend on Him!

In the process of writing this book and putting together "The Nathanael Project" I lost my pastor son. He was only 30 when God called him to Heaven in a similar fashion to his granddad via a traffic accident. I was his dad, he was my son, he was my preacher-boy, my protégée, and my friend. Add to this the fact that Josh was assisting me with this book via critique and helping to develop the Small Group material for "The Nathanael Project." He was the younger eyes I needed to make the program relevant to the next generations.

I miss both greatly—probably more so my son since, as I write this, his loss is still very raw. Both helped shape me into being a better son, father, husband, pastor, speaker and writer. I am eternally grateful for them and long to see them again on the other shore when my work is completed.

To follow is the last article Josh wrote for his congregation (page 181) along with the poem from my dad—"I'm Home Now" (page 183)

Naturally, I am grateful to the love of my life for 40 years, Vonnie. She willingly permitted me to use her in illustrations and was the first-line of proofing. She also encouraged me to keep on keeping on with this project. Her threat to take away the manuscript as I continued to make changes is the reason why it is now in your hands . . . at least the first edition.

Appreciation

Credit must be given to the founder of 800FollowMe, Dick Dean, who, always on the cutting-edge, saw past his initial vision of sharing the Gospel via phone and recognized the value of a Church-Evangelism program. He, along with the Christian Heritage Foundation, afforded me the time to write this book, create "The Nathanael Project" and encouraged me along the way.

I'm indebted to my good friend and colleague, pastor Davis Duggins, for taking my wood, hay and stubble and turning it into something readable. His editorial skills and suggested divisions within the chapters were greatly appreciated and are readily on display in this book.

My college roommate from Indiana, Mike "Duke" Dukate, with whom we were "iron sharpening iron" during those early years and have now reconnected doing the same, not only read through the manuscript but also provided most of the thought-provoking questions at the end of each chapter. And a good friend, Val Macblain from New Mexico, now with the Lord who, despite battling brain cancer, reviewed the book and made constructive comments.

Proofreaders, Shelley Allen, Diane Arnold, Marilyn Bossard (who went through the book twice), Ginny Schoonover and Jewell Utt helped at various stages with the manuscript, for which I am grateful. Pastor Phil Norris did a once-over between the first and second printing. Karen Brightbill's artistic eye did a beautiful job designing the cover and Gillespie Printing in Allentown, Pennsylvania, not only gave me a good price but did a fine job.

I stand on the shoulders of others, especially evangelists like Jack Wyrtzen and Percy Crawford, from Word of Life and Pinebrook, respectively, along with Jerry Falwell whose ministries impacted my life. Church evangelist Wendell Calder and missiologist and Professor Ron Blue counseled me during this project and were contributors. There are too many pastors to mention who were encouragers, although Pastor Jim Carver made a helpful critique between the first and second printing. I'm also beholden to Elmer Towns, for his words of encouragement as I began this project and for writing the forward.

I would be remiss if I didn't thank all the prayer partners Vonnie and I have. You all know who you are and must know that your prayer support greatly aided me.

Special note of thanks goes to Lyle Hartzell and the Word of Life Inn staff for allowing me to set up a writing shop on the second floor of a chalet somewhat overlooking the lake at Schroon Lake, NY (I had to place a mirror on a chair so that I could actually see the lake). Those few weeks, however, were huge in helping me formulate the content for this book.

My sound guy, Dave Hinson, who always makes me sound great as he deletes all my "ahs," ums," and unnerving loud gasps for air between sentences, was a huge encouragement during this process and made the audio book possible.

And thanks to one of my best friends, Bruce Martin, who allowed me to bounce off ideas and often threw them back with a greater perspective.

Finally, I thank my Father in Heaven who has given me gifts and abilities and placed on my heart this eternally worthy cause of sharing one's faith. May His Kingdom be added to and advanced from those who take to heart what is written in this book, who share the greatest story ever told about the greatest Person to ever live concerning the greatest gift ever offered.

Dan & Vonnie Allen (2016)

Is Christ Enough?
by Pastor Joshua Allen
Philippians 3

Is Christ enough? That was the question I asked myself as I drove along the Organ Mountains late Sunday night (Las Cruces, NM). I like to drive. It's what I do when I am trying to think or work through an issue. Some people walk, others journal, for me the times I feel closest to God is when I am driving. I usually will get in the car and start driving, windows down, radio off, just me, the road, and God.

One of my favorite drives is the road that runs parallel to the Organ Mountains. I love this road for two reasons: 1) it is usually free from other cars, 2) you can see the beauty and power of the mountains while driving on it. The mountains remind me of the beauty of God and also Moses at Mount Sinai. I know we have the Holy Spirit in our lives and can pray anywhere but for me at the Organ Mountains I feel closer to God. So I go there often, drive and pray.

That is where I found myself late Sunday night. As I drove and talked with God, one prevailing question kept coming to mind: Is Christ enough? The reason for this thought I think comes from the last two sermons on Philippians 3 about the Apostle Paul's desire that Christ be enough. Paul in this chapter puts Christ at the forefront and in the end ultimately says, nothing else matters but Christ. So we as Christians are to follow Christ with everything and as Christians we should probably ask ourselves often, is Christ enough?

You may be wondering why someone who just preached the last two sermons would be asking that question. Wouldn't I have already worked through it myself? Well yes and no, the truth is, that the majority of the time, while I believe sermons are for the church as a whole, they are also for me. I use them often to preach to myself just as much as I am preaching to the rest of the body of Christ and sometimes it means I have to personally work through some application points after the sermon.

So I drove, late in the night, after preaching that day on Philippians 3, praying and talking with God, and the prevailing question was: is Christ enough? Is his work enough, or do I want more, do I seek my own will, or my own desires, or do I make it more about myself than I make it about Him? It's a tough question, and it is even a harder question to answer. But my prayer is what Paul said earlier in Philippians 1:21 that *For me to live is Christ, and to die is gain.*

I think Paul writes this not only as a reminder for the church of Philippi but a reminder for himself, a reminder to ask the question, is Christ enough? We need to ask ourselves this question often, whether it be driving along the Organ Mountains, sitting in a chair journaling, kneeling down to pray, or whatever way you feel closest to God.

Is Christ enough? I want Him to be, that is why I continue to look at Scripture and learn, that is why I continue to drive and ask, not because I have already obtained it, but because I want to obtain it. So I drive, I pray, I ask. I pray you do the same so we can all say, *"For me to live is Christ, and to die is gain."*

Josh & Shelley Allen (2013)

"I'm Home Now"©

Rev. Russell T. Allen

I'm in my eternal home now! It's all true! This place is absolutely magnificent. Human words cannot explain it, and I'm so alive, so free, so happy, so perfectly content.

I'm Home Now! My mind is clear, all pain is gone, my hopes and dreams have all been satisfied the moment I left earth's shores and landed here in Heaven.

Thank God *I'm home now*! There are no misunderstandings in this place. No anger, no harsh words, no hurt feelings, no selfish acts, no problems on my part or that of others. I see plainly here and although God's will was sometimes hard for me to see on earth, here it is beautifully perceived.

Praise the Lord, *I'm home now*! Sorrow is foreign to this place and I have yet to see anyone weeping. And the friends that I have met, you wouldn't believe. And they seem so different and so gracious. I'll probably spend half of eternity talking to them.

I'm home now! The greatest thrill was to see my Savior— face to face. If I could cry, I would, but I'm just consumed with such joy and love that it defies comprehension. Mortals on earth cannot know it, it is just unexplainable.

I'm home now! I'm filled with God's glory and with his radiance. I've found that talking to people on earth about Jesus has made the inhabitants of this place extremely delighted. They said I would meet some of those I brought to the Savior later on. That gave me rapture because I now know what this abode is like.

So, *I'm home now*!

If I could speak from this side I would say that the old adage is never out of date. It goes: "Only one life, it will soon be past, only what's done for Christ will last." And in parting let me say, don't ever pity me, or shed bitter tears . . . I'm better off now than in all my earthly years. I've started my new life and it's been worth it all. I trust I'll meet you again here. Maranatha! *I'm home now*!

The Nathanael Project

Everybody has a Nathanael

www.TheNathanaelProject.com

"The Nathanael Project" is a 2-month-long (9 Sunday) church-evangelism program that includes everyone in your church—from children in Primary and Junior Church, to teens and adults. The program consists of an easy-to-read book on evangelism: *Exhaling the Gospel of Jesus Christ . . . Evangelism as Natural as Breathing the Truth*; a daily & family devotional booklet which also includes the Small Group guide; curriculums for children and teens; lessons for Adult Sunday School and Small Groups; a short video for each Small Group session as well as sermons for the pastor. The goal is for everyone to pray for, and learn how to share Jesus with, their Nathanael (friend, co-worker, class-mate, neighbor, relative), because "Everyone Has a Nathanael" . . . someone who needs to be brought to Jesus (John 1:45).